Yale Language Series

Faculty Guide to Japanese: The Spoken Language Multimedia Collection

Mari Noda

Yale University Press
New Haven and London

Printed in the United States of America.

ISBN   0-300-07496-4 Japanese:
        The Spoken Language Interactive
        CD-ROM Program—Macintosh
ISBN   0-300-07563-4 Japanese:
        The Spoken Language Interactive
        CD-ROM Program—PC
ISBN   0-300-07562-6 User's Guide to
        Japanese: The Spoken Language
        Interactive CD-ROM Program—paper

Library of Congress Cataloguing-in-Publication Data
Noda, Mari.
    Faculty guide to Japanese: the spoken language
multimedia collection / Mari Noda.
    p. cm. — (Yale language series)
    Includes index.
    ISBN 0-300-07568-5 (alk. paper)
    1. Japanese language—Study and teaching—Foreign
speakers—audiovisual aids. 2. Japanese language—
Spoken Japanese—Study and teaching. 3. Educators—
United States—Handbooks, manuals, etc. I. Title.
II. Series.
    PL519.N58   1998
    495.6'8007—dc21   97-39351
                              CIP
A catalogue record for this book is available from the
British Library.

The paper in this book meets the guidelines for permanence
and durability of the Committee on Production Guidelines
for Book Longevity of the Council on Library Resources.

10 9 8 7 6 5 4 3 2 1

CONTENTS

SECTION 1: THE LEARNING ENVIRONMENT AND THE
SHARING OF RESPONSIBILITY 1

SHARING RESPONSIBILITIES FOR LEARNING....................................1
COMPONENTS OF *JSL-MC*..4
   Interactive CD-ROM Program 4
   User's Guide and *Faculty Guide*..4
   Textbook 5
   Audiocassettes 5
   Videocassette of Core Conversations 6
   A Question and Answer Supplement 6
   Teacher's Supplement 6
   Culture Videos...7
INTENDED LEARNERS 8
   Experienced Learners 9
   Young Learners..9
   Learners Whose Native Language Is Not English....................... 10
ACCESSIBILITY.. 10

SECTION 2: PERFORMING IN JAPANESE: FROM
REHEARSAL TO IMPROVISATION 14

OBJECTIVES... 14
ASSUMPTIONS 15
PERFORMANCE OF CORE CONVERSATIONS (CCS) IN CONTEXT......... 15
   Considering the Basic Context for Conversation Performance 16
   Preparing Necessary Props and Placing Them 17
   Re-creating the Particular Relationship Represented in the CC..... 17
   Planning How the Conversation Might Begin and End 17
   Varying the Basic Context to Elicit CC Variation 18
   Eliciting Student Performance... 19
   Expanding the CC 21
   Varying the CC 23
   Asking Content Questions 25
EXTENDED DISCOURSE EXERCISES... 27
MODIFICATIONS THROUGH ERROR CORRECTION DURING REHEARSED
ACTIVITIES 29

SECTION 3: DISCUSSION SESSIONS: LANGUAGE LEARNING, CULTURE, AND LANGUAGE 33

OBJECTIVES 33
DISCUSSION ABOUT LANGUAGE LEARNING 34
  Program Goals and Course Objectives 34
  Learning Strategies 35
CULTURE IN THE LANGUAGE PROGRAM 36
DISCUSSING BEHAVIORAL CULTURE USING CC VIDEO SEGMENTS ... 38
  Silent Viewing of a CC 38
  Viewing the CC with Sound 39
DISCUSSING INFORMATIONAL CULTURE USING CULTURE VIDEOS 40
DISCUSSING LANGUAGE FORMS IN CULTURAL CONTEXTS 41
  CC Translation (Optional) 42
  CC Notes and Transcription 42
  Structural Patterns 43

SECTION 4: REHEARSING IN CLASS WITH MULTIMEDIA TOOLS 45

OBJECTIVES 45
CC VOCABULARY AND BUILD-UP PRACTICE WITH THE CD-ROM PROGRAM OR AUDIOTAPES 46
CC ROLE PLAY WITH THE CD-ROM PROGRAM OR CC VIDEO 48
DRILLS WITH THE CD-ROM PROGRAM 48
UTILIZATION WITH THE CD-ROM PROGRAM 51

SECTION 5: ASSESSMENT STRATEGIES: TASKS AND PROCEDURES 54

REHEARSED ORAL INTERACTION (CC CHECK) 54
STRUCTURE (DRILLS, SPS, STRUCTURE CHECK) 55
  Drill Check (the CD-ROM Program or Audiotapes) 55
  Structural Pattern Questioning (the CD-ROM Program or A Question and Answer Supplement) 56
  Structure Check with the CD-ROM Program 57
COMPREHENSION 57
SIMULATION USING UTILIZATION 58
MONITORING STUDENT LEARNING 59
  Activating the Record Session Information Function 59
  Type of Data Recorded 59
THE ORAL INTERVIEW 60
  Scripting an Oral Interview 60
  Eliciting a Meaningful Performance in an Oral Interview 62

Giving Feedback on an Oral Interview 63

SECTION 6: USING CULTURE VIDEOS IN THE LANGUAGE
CLASS 64

INTEGRATION 64
PROCEDURES FOR DISCUSSION OF CULTURE VIDEOS 66
Previewing Discussion 66
Viewing the Culture Video 66
Postviewing Discussion 66
Practice Activities in Japanese 67
CULTURE VIDEO TOPICS FOR DISCUSSION AND COMMUNICATIVE
PRACTICE 67
Meiji: Asia's Response to the West (*The Pacific Century* #2) 68
Reinventing Japan (*The Pacific Century* #5) 70
Inside Japan, Inc. (*The Pacific Century* #6) 71
Videos from *Faces of Japan II* 72
SAMPLE VIDEO WORKSHEETS 74

SECTION 7: PACING: SAMPLE HOURLY ASSIGNMENTS 83

GETTING STARTED 83
Classroom Instructions 84
Greetings and Useful Phrases 86
Pronunciation Practice 88
Orientation 88
COORDINATING SCRIPT-BASED PERFORMANCE AND APPLICATION 90

SECTION 8: ACTIVITIES FOR ADVANCED STUDENTS:
EXPANDING A DISCOURSE REPERTOIRE 92

CC REPORTING 92
CC RESTATEMENT 94
PRESENTATIONS BASED ON CULTURE VIDEO TOPICS 97

INDEX 101

SECTION 1:
THE LEARNING ENVIRONMENT AND THE SHARING OF RESPONSIBILITY

Japanese: The Spoken Language, Multimedia Collection (JSL-MC) is a comprehensive learning tool that supports approximately 150 hours of instruction in the Japanese language at the introductory level. It is suitable for individuals who are serious about learning to interact with the Japanese through oral communication. While comprehensive enough to support self-study by individuals, it is most effective when used as an integral part of a structured curriculum in a formal learning environment. Using video and audio materials and an interactive computer program, teachers can introduce Japanese language and culture in a more dynamic manner than is possible with textbooks alone.

This chapter describes the principal elements that shape a learning environment and suggests how *JSL-MC* supports one that is effective. It outlines the component parts of *JSL-MC*, discusses the question of necessary equipment, describes the users who are likely to benefit from this multimedia collection, and addresses the learning strategies appropriate to the material.

SHARING RESPONSIBILITIES FOR LEARNING

How learning of a foreign language proceeds depends on a number of interrelated factors. The plan for integrating the different elements that compose a learning environment is called the curriculum. Within a given foreign language learning environment, the teachers, learners, and materials share curriculum responsibilities in promoting the goals of learning. Teachers, taking advantage of their knowledge about learners, select or create materials to support learning, and they organize activities to engage learners in this process. The materials present the target language and offer suggestions for practice activities. Ultimately, however, it is the learners who have to take responsibility for learning, since no teacher,

1

however dedicated, can learn on their behalf, and no materials, however superior, can help a learner who does not take advantage of their availability. Depending on the design of the curriculum, the relative amount of responsibility each of these three components assumes differs. In addition, external factors such as time, space, and accessibility, in particular, can influence the design.

A program may have a well-balanced level of responsibility-sharing among learners, teachers, and materials. Learners in such an environment are expected to do basic work on their own using the instructional materials. Basic work may involve familiarizing oneself with facts about Japanese language and culture through reading textbooks and viewing videos, and performing the kind of basic practice that helps develop the linguistic skills necessary for language use. For reinforcement, the teacher designs classroom exercises that promote the learners' communicative skills. Even when responsibilities are appropriately divided among teachers, learners, and materials, however, limitations in time or space for their interaction or limitations in the learners' accessibility to materials or teachers slow down learning.

In another type of setting, the teacher has a greater share of responsibility than the materials; in some cases, the teacher supervises much of the interaction between learners and materials. An increased amount of student-teacher interaction should have a positive result, but in reality the student-teacher ratio is often too great for the teacher to give the required amount of individualized attention to every learner. This imbalance results in an excess of time devoted to basic skill practice and information transfer and a loss of adequate time for crucially important contextualized exercises.

Now, consider a different situation. If a greater share of responsibility is borne by more comprehensive materials, the teacher can be freed from most of the mechanical activities required for basic skill acquisition. In such cases, student-teacher interaction can center around highly contextualized, and culturally authentic activities. In other words, the less class time available to the teacher, or the less time the teacher is accessible to the learner, the more the learner will have to depend on the materials to develop basic skills and acquire knowledge about language use.

Such an instructional organization has often been regarded as a deficient model because teacher involvement is less comprehensive. Actually, it constitutes an ideal mode of instruction as long as the teacher devotes most class time to activities that can never be performed by a machine. Only the live instructor can take the learner from the level of basic, automatic linguistic practice to truly communicative, culturally coherent interaction in the target language.

This kind of organization also encourages learners to manage their own learning. Inasmuch as the learning of a language (foreign or native) is likely to continue throughout one's lifetime, even though formal instruction typically lasts only a few years, self-managed learning is a crucially important skill. Learners need to develop strategies for learning that will enable them to continue to progress on their own beyond formal instructional programs. This concept of lifelong learning is especially important for a language such as Japanese, one of the most time-consuming languages to learn for native English speakers with American cultural background.[1] *JSL-MC* may be used in any of these different learning environments, including the one in which learners gain basic linguistic skills and cultural knowledge through self-managed study and have practice in communicative interaction with their teachers.

---

[1]Japanese is one of the Category Four languages, according to the Foreign Service Institute (FSI) classification. To reach the level of proficiency in which the learner can handle most basic daily conversational situations, the average American learner spends more than 1,400 class hours in an intensive setting, as opposed to about 250 hours of instruction in Category One languages, including Spanish, Swahili, and French.

COMPONENTS OF *JSL-MC*

JSL-MC consists of nine sets of interrelated but distinct materials. It may be used alone to concentrate exclusively on the spoken language or, after Lesson 2, in combination with additional materials for instruction in the written language.

Interactive CD-ROM Program

Japanese: The Spoken Language *Interactive CD-ROM Program* (Yale University Press, 1998) is a set of two CD-ROMs, available in both Macintosh and PC formats. Based on *Japanese: The Spoken Language, Part 1 (JSL 1)* by Eleanor Harz Jorden with Mari Noda (Yale University Press, 1987), it provides varied and extensive practice activities to promote the development of competence in spoken Japanese. The 125 Core Conversations are presented in movie form with accompanying analysis. More than 3,500 illustrations with animation provide conversational contexts for practice activities. In addition, some 9,000 sound files offer a rich array of language used in wide-ranging cultural contexts. All examples are authentic, meaningful exchanges, represent-ative of actual interaction with the Japanese.

User's Guide and Faculty Guide

User's Guide to Japanese: The Spoken Language *Interactive CD-Program* (by Mari Noda, Yale University Press, 1998) and this *Faculty Guide to* Japanese: The Spoken Language *Multimedia Collection* offer explanations of how to use *JSL-MC* effectively. A detailed description of the use of the CD-ROM program, along with many helpful hints for self-study learners, is included in the *User's Guide*; this *Faculty Guide* describes in greater detail procedures for implementing *JSL-MC* in a program of instruction.

Textbook

Japanese: The Spoken Language, Part 1 (JSL 1), by Eleanor Harz Jorden with Mari Noda (Yale University Press, 1987), is the first in a three-volume series and contains the initial twelve lessons of the thirty in the series. It provides a systematic introduction to the spoken language in authentic cultural contexts. Taking advantage of the cognitive capabilities of the learner, it combines basic drills for practice of forms with highly contextualized exercises for situation-based activities. The learner builds a linguistic repertoire, step-by-step, and constantly reviews it in spiral fashion. The textbook contains Japanese-English and English-Japanese glossaries as well as an index of key concepts introduced in the twelve lessons. Every Japanese example included in the textbook is presented with accent and intonation marks.

With the help of this textbook, the learner can develop an understanding of the Japanese language as a system of communication in Japanese society. It also serves as a reference work for both learners and teachers.

Audiocassettes

Fourteen audiocassettes, *Japanese: The Spoken Language, Part 1 Revised Tape Series* by Eleanor Harz Jorden and Mari Noda (Cheng & Tsui Company, 1997), are another component of *JSL-MC*. These tapes include recordings of all the Core Conversations, Drills, and Eavesdropping selections from all twelve lessons of *JSL 1*. In addition, an English voice leads the learner through the various activities associated with each Core Conversation as well as with each of the Drills in the first four lessons. All Drills are response drills, with each example constituting a minimal conversation that exemplifies a particular linguistic pattern.

A cassette tape player is more portable than the computer needed for the use of the CD-ROM program. These audiocassettes are useful for developing the learner's ability to control linguistic forms with accurate pronunciation without reference to visual aids.

Videocassette of Core Conversations

Japanese: The Spoken Language, Part 1 Video by Eleanor Harz Jorden and Mari Noda (Cheng & Tsui Company, 1987) includes the 125 Core Conversations in *JSL 1*. It was filmed on location in Tokyo by a professional Japanese production crew headed by a Japanese director. Key characters, even Americans living in Japan, are portrayed by Japanese actors, providing the best models possible for pronunciation and interactional behavior. The people they portray are presumed to be of Asian origin, sharing physical characteristics with typical Japanese.

The audiocassette set and the videocassette may be ordered from Cheng & Tsui Company, P.O. Box 576, Williston, VT 05495; customer service phone 800-554-1964 (http://hoshi.cis.sfu.ca/cheng-tsui). They are also available from The Annenberg/CPB Project, 901 E Street, NW, Washington, DC 20004-2037; phone 202-879-9600 (http://www.learner.org).

A Question and Answer Supplement

A Question and Answer Supplement to Japanese: The Spoken Language, Part 1 (Eleanor Harz Jorden with Mari Noda, Yale University Press, 1994) presents the Structural Patterns of the textbook in a question-and-answer format. All of the questions from this *Supplement* are included in the CD-ROM program, but for many of the questions the *Supplement* provides more detailed answers and more examples than the CD-ROM program. The compact 138-page *Supplement* is easy to carry and use anywhere and requires no equipment.

Teacher's Supplement

Japanese: The Spoken Language, Supplement to Part 1— Japanese Typescript (Eleanor Harz Jorden and Mari Noda, Yale University Press, 1988), or the *Teacher's Supplement*, contains the scripts for all the Core Conversations and Drills of *JSL 1*, written in normal Japanese orthography. Since *JSL* focuses on teaching the spoken language, learners are expected to use the oral segments on the audiotapes and the CD-ROM program as their models. Romanization, which is used in the textbook, CD-ROM program, and *A Question and Answer Supplement*, is introduced not for reading or writing but only as a reminder of what has already been heard many times. In contrast, the Japanese contained in the *Teacher's Supplement* is a script for teachers already proficient in Japanese, spoken and written, who find the familiar Japanese script easier to read, and who are already able to pronounce spoken Japanese accurately without recorded models. It is not an instructional text appropriate for learners studying the Japanese writing system.

Culture Videos

In the learning of a foreign language, knowledge about the history of the target culture does not directly enhance competence in that language. Knowledge of history and the society in which the language is used, however, can certainly enrich one's understanding of the way people think and behave in the target culture. The eight culture videos included in *JSL-MC* are a rich source of information about Japan and are excellent as instruments for motivating language learners. The videos included in *JSL-MC* are:

Culture Videos from *the Pacific Century* Series (the Annenberg/CPB Project, 1992, running time: 60 minutes each)

1. "Meiji: Asia's Response to the West" (*The Pacific Century* #2)

2. "Reinventing Japan" (*The Pacific Century* #5)

3. "Inside Japan, Inc." (*The Pacific Century* #6)

Culture Videos from *Faces of Japan II* Series (Pacific Mountain Network, 1990, running time: 15 minutes each)

4. "Puppeteer's Apprentice (*Bunraku* Puppeteer)" (*Faces of Japan II* #1)

5. "An American Portrait (*Sumo* Wrestler)" (*Faces of Japan II* #2)

6. "Frontier Fisherman" (*Faces of Japan II* #3)

7. "Woman Soldier" (*Faces of Japan II* #4)

8. "Cram School" (*Faces of Japan II* #5)

Of these culture videos, those from the *Pacific Century* series represent a slightly higher academic level of difficulty; they are particularly interesting for the learner who is interested in history. The *Faces of Japan II* tapes appeal to all audiences, even those as young as middle school students. The latter series has an accompanying teacher's guide (*A Teacher's Guide to Faces of Japan II* by Jacquelyn Johnson and Lynn Parisi, Lakewood, CO: Pacific Mountain Network, 1990), that provides program summaries, objectives, topics for discussion before and after viewing each video, and background notes for the teacher.

All culture videos are available from The Annenberg/CPB Project, 901 E Street, NW, Washington, DC 20004-2037; phone 202-879-9600 (http://www.learner.org).

INTENDED LEARNERS

JSL-MC is aimed primarily at beginning learners of Japanese in high schools, colleges, and places of employment, whether they are enrolled in a regular course of study or learning through self-study. Learners are assumed to have an American linguistic and cultural background, but other types of learners can also take advantage of *JSL-MC* in ways described here.

Experienced Learners

JSL-MC introduces the various features of spoken Japanese in a systematic, step-by-step fashion, allowing learners to develop a solid foundation for oral communication. It can also be used for review and assessment and as a resource for more advanced learners. Depending on the type of experience these nonbeginners have had, their needs will differ. Some have an extensive vocabulary but lack the ability to put words and phrases together for effective communication. Others have a good understanding of structure but lack the ability to take part in effective social interaction because they have never learned the politeness and formality levels that are a crucially important aspect of communication in Japanese. Still others need to work on oral delivery. Each of these various needs can be met by assigning different activities in *JSL-MC* to students according to their background. See Section 8 for examples of classroom activities for advanced learners of Japanese. See also the *User's Guide* for ways to use *JSL-MC* for review.

Young Learners

JSL-MC is intended for learners who are cognitively and socially mature. Very young learners will find many of the explanations in the textbook and *A Question and Answer Supplement* to be too complex. The Core Conversation videos of *JSL-MC*, however, may be used for comprehension exercises as long as it is made clear to the observers that the speech styles are those of adults. The Core Conversations depict a wide variety of settings, including shops, restaurants, business offices, campuses, seminar rooms, street scenes, hotel lobbies, and homes. Abundant illustrations and graphics in the CD-ROM program make some of the learning accessible to young learners. Also, as was previously pointed out, some of the culture videos are appropriate for middle school classes.

Learners Whose Native Language Is Not English

JSL-MC is best suited for learners who have an American cultural background and who speak English as a native language. Depending on their proficiency in English, nonnative speakers of English may find some of the English explanations of structure, particularly those in the textbook, difficult to understand. Explanations in *A Question and Answer Supplement* and in the CD-ROM program are easier to grasp. These learners can also take advantage of the video presentations of the Core Conversations and the extensive practice activities in *JSL-MC*, for these activities do not rely on translation. In particular, the CD-ROM program incorporates video and graphic images to accompany these practice activities, further reducing the need to use English. The culture videos are helpful in giving these learners an opportunity to listen to English narration with aid from visual images.

ACCESSIBILITY

Depending on the accessibility of various types of equipment, different components of *JSL-MC* can be used in and out of class, as shown in Figure 1-1.

Figure 1-1
The Use of *JSL-MC* Components, Depending on Accessibility

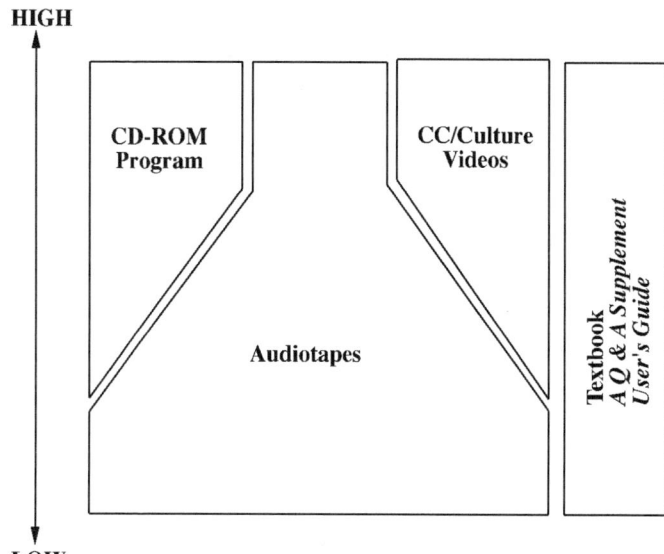

The printed components of *JSL-MC*, i.e., the textbook, *A Question and Answer Supplement*, and the *User's Guide*, are available for use and do not depend on technological equipment. Even with limited equipment, most students today have some access to an audiocassette player, so audiotapes should be used extensively in the absence of computer equipment or a video cassette recorder (VCR). In some educational programs, students have limited or no access to computers outside of class, but the teacher is able to use the CD-ROM program in class to enhance classroom activities. As equipment accessibility increases, we can expect students to use the CD-ROM program and video materials outside of class to a greater degree, whereas the heavy reliance on audiotapes is likely to decrease. However, even with widespread accessibility to high-technology equipment, audiotapes continue to be extremely useful for supporting oral language practice without visual aids.

The type of classroom activities will reflect the use of the different components of *JSL-MC*, as determined by

the degree of equipment accessibility (shown in
Figure 1-2).

**Figure 1-2
The Use of *JSL-MC* Components in
Various Settings**

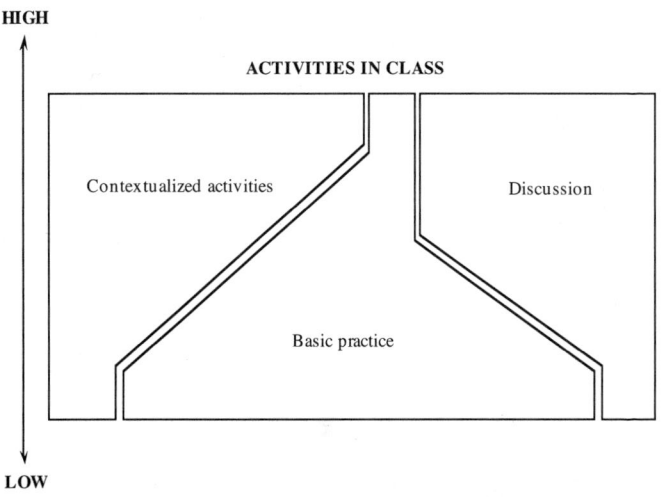

A severe limitation on equipment use will restrict
classroom activities to more basic practice in developing
linguistic skills, thus slowing down the general pace of
learning. Even at the lower level of equipment accessibility,
however, some class time should be reserved for contextualized activities and discussion about Japanese and learning
Japanese. As the accessibility to equipment increases,
students can prepare for class using a wider range of
multimedia tools on their own. Teachers can use class time
for contextualized exercises which do not require the use of
multimedia tools. The CD-ROM program and video
materials may be used in class for the purpose of discussion, assessment, and review. In some programs, teachers
may also use the Internet to disseminate course syllabi,
schedules, and other information relating to the language
program. The use of additional technology such as the
Internet and videoconferencing greatly expands the
availability of Japanese instruction, especially given so
comprehensive a learning tool as *JSL-MC*.

The amount of time students study Japanese outside of class has a marked effect on curriculum design, similar to that of the accessibility of equipment. Time and accessibility are mutually dependent in that even with time, students can do only a limited amount of work without access to technological equipment. Conversely, even with ready access to equipment, students with insufficient time can do little to prepare for class and, as a result, may become more teacher-dependent.

The next three chapters discuss in greater detail three major types of classroom activities. These are (1) contextualized activities based on extensive multimedia learning outside of class, (2) discussion, and (3) more basic practice of linguistic forms using multimedia tools.

SECTION 2:
PERFORMING IN JAPANESE: FROM REHEARSAL TO IMPROVISATION

This chapter provides concrete examples of activities that assume extensive student use of the practice components of *JSL-MC* outside of class. (See the *User's Guide* for procedures students are expected to follow.) These are activities that require students to perform interactions in Japanese using the linguistic and cultural skills and knowledge they have gained through their self-study.

The examples given in this *Faculty Guide* by no means exhaust the variety of activities that you can do in the classroom. You may also develop additional types of exercises and, depending on local conditions such as the physical layout of the classroom, the size of the class, and students' backgrounds, adjust the activities suggested here. The romanization used follows that of *JSL 1*. See the textbook and *User's Guide* for discussion of this romanization.

OBJECTIVES

The primary objective of situational exercises is to help learners apply their skills in Japanese interaction. Students are expected to use basic linguistic skills, such as accurate pronunciation, appropriate word choice, structural accuracy, and an ability to construct coherent discourse; to express themselves effectively; and to interpret intentions within communicative interactions. By themselves, these skills are not sufficient for effective communication; the ability to analyze a situation of interaction swiftly and respond to it with the appropriate linguistic activity is also required.

Performance of Core Conversations (CCs) in class helps students make the connection between the particular CCs they have practiced with the contexts in which they may occur, and modify an actual performance as needed. In addition, CCs are used as an anchor point for building a repertoire of performances. Manipulations such as substitution of appropriate vocabulary items, changes in the relationship between the participants, and expansion of the conversation in different directions will contribute to the building of students' repertoires. Communicative activities based on Drills, Structural Patterns, and Utilization provide learners with the opportunity to use the short exchanges they have learned within extended discourse in shifting contexts.

Assumptions

Performance of any kind requires rehearsal—practice of a fixed script—at different levels. CC performance involves an execution of rehearsed lines in context. It also requires understanding the situation in which the conversation occurs and what the speakers accomplish by their participation in the conversation. The activities outlined here assume that students have access to the CD-ROM program or the CC videos and audiotapes and have used them to prepare for class. The classroom activities themselves do not include the use of these tools. However, if students are not prepared and are not ready to perform the assigned CC or engage in extended discourse that assumes control of the Drills and Utilization, you will need to modify the contextualized activities described in the following sections to include more basic practice of linguistic forms as suggested in Section 4.

Performance of Core Conversations (CCs) in Context

The video segment of a CC provides much information about the conversation's context. This information is reinforced and amplified in the Setting and Notes sections of the CD-ROM program and the Miscellaneous Notes in the textbook. Let's consider a CC from Lesson 2B and go through the recommended steps to prepare for and implement its contextualized performance. The conversation is as follows:

(N)	(J)
a. **Nan desu ka./**	a. **Dore desu ka./**
b. **Sore desu.**	b. **Aa, kore desu ka.**
	Zisyo desu yo./

J refers to a native speaker of Japanese, and N to a nonnative.

Considering the Basic Context for Conversation Performance

The most practical way to interpret the word *context* is to think about where, when, to whom, in whose presence, and why the speakers say what they say.

1. Where might such a conversation take place, and who are the speakers?

   In the video segment, two colleagues, Mr. Carter and Mr. Suzuki of the Continental Bank, are meeting in an informal restaurant, probably after work. The same conversation could take place in a number of places where two colleagues might meet and engage in small talk, including an office, a classroom, or the street.

2. What makes N ask the first question?

   N must not be able to tell what the object is. In the video, J places a wrapped object next to him as he sits down. The relationship between J and N must be such that N feels comfortable asking this question of J.

3. Why does J answer the question with another question?

   N has not made clear in his question what he is talking about, so J needs to clarify. Note that in the video, N does not point to the object with his finger.

4. Why does N use **sore** in identifying what he is talking about?

The object is closer to J than it is to N. J's switch to the use of **kore** in reference to the same object confirms its location. On the video, the object is in fact right next to J.

5. Why does J use sentence particle **yo** in the last line?

   J knows that it's a dictionary, and assumes that this is new information for N.

6. Why are the speakers using the **desu/-masu** style of speech?

   N and J are colleagues at the same workplace, but they observe a certain amount of social distance from one another.

Preparing Necessary Props and Placing Them

Think of body movements and props that will make the interaction authentic. For this CC, you will need a dictionary, which should be wrapped or placed in a bag to conceal its identity. To practice the supplementary vocabulary, you will also need a book, a magazine, and a newspaper. The items should be placed in bags or wrapped and placed near the person who will play the role of J.

Re-creating the Particular Relationship Represented in the CC

To identify the two speakers as coworkers, you might indicate that all students are working for one particular company. The same conversation can take place in a number of different places, so you need not identify the location as a restaurant.

Planning How the Conversation Might Begin and End

A CC does not always represent a complete conversation; usually, it is only a small segment of a longer conversation. If possible, plan what might normally be said or done before the first line and after the last line of the CC, i.e., what primes the occurrence of the CC and what might be said to bring the conversation to closure. In many instances, inclusion of these starting and closing lines will serve as a useful review of previously learned materials.

In the particular example just given, the conversation might start when one conversation partner enters the scene holding an unidentified object. At the end of the CC, it is likely that an acknowledgment, such as **Aa, zisyo desu ka.**, or some other comment follows the last line.

Varying the Basic Context to Elicit CC Variation

- Identify the structural patterns and vocabulary that the CC introduces. To do this, refer to the Breakdowns section in the textbook or in the *Teacher's Supplement*. New patterns that are explained in the Structural Patterns (SP) section are indicated in the Breakdowns section by the SP number in parentheses. Supplementary vocabulary items are marked with a plus (+) sign.

  The preceding CC introduces the first example of the **ko-so-a-do** series and rhetorical questions such as **Aa, sore desu ka.**, used to confirm the speaker's understanding of the topic of the conversation at the given moment. The **ko-so-a-do** series is explained in SP1. The rhetorical check question is explained in the Miscellaneous Notes in the textbook and in the Notes in the CD-ROM program. There are three supplementary vocabulary items: **hon, zassi,** and **sinbun**.

- Plan elicitation methods. Practicing the use of **kore** versus **sore** will require clear placement of the object used as the topic of discussion. You will also need to change the identity of the items to elicit the supplementary vocabulary items. When appropriate, require the use of a rhetorical check question; otherwise, students simply will not use it.

Eliciting Student Performance

Having prepared the props and made the plans for priming the CC, you can implement your plan. Note that in the planning stage, you analyzed the language of the CC to establish the appropriate context of its occurrence. In eliciting performance from the students, this process is reversed: You present the context so that students recall the language they can use in the given context.

- Prime the conversation.

  You can show the video segment of the CC using a videocassette or the CD-ROM program. For a more highly contextualized application, place a wrapped dictionary in front of one student (S1). Pointing at the object, you may say to another student (S2), **Sumimasen, S1-san ni kiite kudasai.** (These expressions are introduced in Greetings and Useful Phrases in the Introduction section.) If the students have learned the CC at home, this short priming will elicit the CC from S1 and S2 as shown in Figure 2-1.

Figure 2-1
CC Initiated

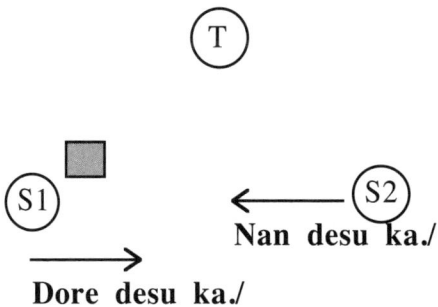

To help S2 further, you (T) may place a card with a large question mark on the object as you prompt S2. Note that you never have to model the full dialogue, and students need not assume the generic roles of J and N. It is clear from the priming context which student should say J's part.

Another way to prime a CC performance is for the teacher to assume the role of one of the speakers. This approach gives the teacher tighter control over the development of the CC and provides a better method when the conversation or the context is more complex.

- Practice supplementary vocabulary in the context of the CC.

- For the example CC given, use a book, a magazine, or a newspaper instead of a dictionary to elicit **hon**, **zassi**, or **sinbun**. Place each of these items in a bag, showing the contents to only one of the participating students. Have students practice these items in context, rather than as isolated words.

- Practice the new structural patterns in context by varying the placement of the object as illustrated in Figures 2-2 to 2-4.

Figure 2-2
Basic Placement of Objects

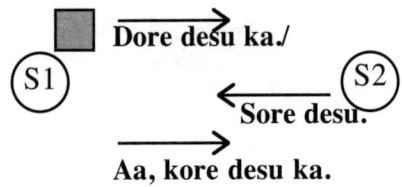

Figure 2-3
Placement of Objects for Variation 1

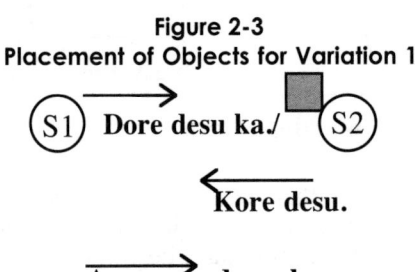

Figure 2-4
Placement of Objects for Variation 2

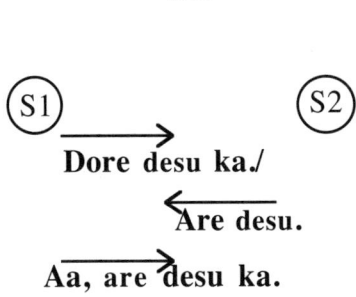

The second variation (Figure 2-4) is possible once the word **are** (in the next CC) is introduced. Begin to incorporate these variations as soon as students can perform the CC in its basic form. Develop the conversation to a more spontaneous level by making only one change at a time and gradually increasing the number of variables.

Expanding the CC

As pointed out earlier, you can expand the example CC by having N add a comment about the object once its identity is revealed. Thus:

(N)   (J)

a. **Nan desu ka./**   a. **Dore desu ka./**

b. **Sore desu.**   b. **Aa, kore desu ka.**
                                   Zisyo desu yo./

c. **Aa, zisyo desu ka.**

Notice that the expansion adds natural closure to this conversation. It also provides students with the opportunity to practice the /X **desu**/ pattern again with nominals (nouns) other than **ko-so-a-do** words.

You can play the role of one of the speakers to demonstrate the example closure, and then have students practice it. Encourage students to use other possible ways of closing this conversation (e.g., **Aa, soo desu ka.**) using recently learned expressions.

You can also expand a CC by adding an introductory portion. Consider Lesson 7A, CC3. In this CC, N is visiting J's office and is trying to find some people who work in that office.

(N)		(J)	
a.	**Nakamura-san irassyaimasu ka./**	a.	**Ima tyotto orimasen ga..**
b.	**Zyaa, Nisida-san wa?**	b.	**Nisida desu ka./ Nisida wa san- gai ni orimasu ga..**
c.	**A, soo desu ka. Doo mo.**		

In preparation for the performance of this CC, the teacher might divide the class into two groups, assigning them different office affiliations—Office X and Office Y. Students who belong to Office X assume the role of N; those who belong to Office Y assume the role of J. The teacher assumes the role of a supervisor in Office X and asks a worker to deliver some documents to Mr/s. Nakamura and Mr/s. Nishida in Office Y. Thus, the following lines could be added before the CC:

(N)   (J2)

                         a. **Sumimasen ga, kore, Y no Nakamura-san ni onegai-simasu. Sore kara, kore wa Nisida-san ni.**

Nakamura-san to Nisida-san desu ne. Wakarimasita. Itte mairimasu.   b. **Onegai-simasu. Itte (i)rassyai.**

This introduction has several functions. First, it contextualizes the CC by giving the reason for N's visit to Office Y. It also clarifies the choice of politeness levels the students use in their interaction. They now have clear roles in this overall context.

Second, this sequence primes the CC performance through contextualization. There is now no need to announce to the students that they are to perform the CC. The CC performance is elicited instead.

Third, this opening sequence describes the task in which N is to participate, including the names of the people N is to inquire about. It helps learners recall the conversational content of the CC.

Finally, the added sequence requires the use of expressions that students have just learned in a previous CC of the same lesson—**itte mairimasu**, **itte kimasu**, and **itte (i)rassyai**. Learners will need to choose the more polite **itte mairimasu** by considering the relative social positions of the speakers.

Varying the CC

Varying the CC typically involves an alteration in the conditions under which the conversation occurs. Application Exercise B at the end of Sections A and B of each lesson in the textbook provides concrete suggestions for variation of the CCs in that section. In the example from Lesson 2, you can change the context from one involving an unidentified object to one involving an identified object. The conversation may be altered as follows:

(N)   (J)

a. **Zisyo desu ka./**   a. **Kore desu ka./**

b. **Ee.**   b. **Ee, zisyo desu.**

The overall discourse structure of the conversation is kept, but the intentions expressed in this variation are different from those in the original CC. Notice again that you can elicit the variation not by giving the forms you want students to use but by suggesting a change in the context. Students have to analyze the change and come up with the forms that match the new context.

Another type of alteration of conditions involves a change in the relationship between the speakers or between the speaker and the person who is being talked about. For instance, in the example from Lesson 7, you can change the affiliation of Nakamura and Nishida to elicit a variation such as the following:

(N)   (J)

a. **Nakamura orimasu ka./**   a. **Ima tyotto irassyaimasen ga..**

b. **Zyaa, Nisida wa?**   b. **Nisida-san desu ka./ Nisida-san wa san-gai ni irassyaimasu ga..**

c. **A, soo desu ka. Doo mo.**

This kind of variation exercise is especially important for developing learners' ability to respond smoothly to the conversational situation with an appropriate language level.

CCs in *JSL-MC* begin with the **desu/-masu** speech style but later introduce a more casual style of speech as well. They also introduce polite forms. The importance of these forms goes beyond their function of expressing politeness; they denote the important social distinction of ingroup versus outgroup, i.e., *uchi* versus *soto*, in Japan. In many instances, the forms of politeness signal which person is responsible for the action mentioned or which person is affected by that action. Forms thus play an essential role in making areas of communication clear. As Japanese mature socially, the range of language registers they are expected to handle expands. Variation in CCs helps learners develop the ability to comprehend and use the various registers used by adult speakers of Japanese.

Asking Content Questions

CC performance may be followed by intensive questioning about CC content. This type of practice will become useful starting around Lesson 3. Extensive questioning will be possible only after the extended predicate pattern (the /**no desu**/ pattern) is introduced in Lesson 7B and more fully explained in Lesson 9B. The objectives of content questioning following CC performance are twofold: (1) it reinforces the content of the CC in a different format, and (2) it provides opportunities for students to use previously learned structures and vocabulary in new contexts.

For content questioning, follow these guidelines:

• Use vocabulary and structure already introduced.

• Start with global questions and proceed gradually to details. For example, questions (1) through (3) here are more general questions about various CCs as a whole, whereas (4) through (6) are more detailed questions seeking specific information gathered from particular parts of the conversation.

(1) **Kore wa doko desu ka./**

(2) **Nan no hanasi desu ka./**

(3) **Doo site Suzuki-san wa kono hanasi o sita n desu ka./**

(4) **Miraa-san wa nani o kaimasita ka./**

(5) **Koosyuudenwa wa doko desu ka./**

(6) **Suzuki-san wa nan-zi ni otaku ni kaette imasu ka./**

- Make the questioning sequence conversationally authentic. Sometimes a series of questions can sound like an interrogation. You can do several things to avoid such an effect.

  – Order the questions so that one flows into another smoothly. Avoid frequent jumping from one question to another, unrelated question. Use connecting expressions such as **sore zyaa, de mo**, or **zyaa yappari** to smooth the transitions.

  – Do not repeat the same topic for every question. For example, if the first question asks where Ms. Miller is and the second question asks what she is doing, the topic identifying phrase **Miraa-san wa** should be used only in the first question (**Miraa-san wa doko desu ka./**), and not in the second (**Nani o site iru n desu ka./**). Note the use of the extended predicate ending (**n desu ka./**) in the second question, which can be used only after this pattern has been introduced.

  – Give a natural, conversational reaction to the information students provide in their answers. This can be a simple **Aa, soo desu ka.** or **Soo datta n desu ka.** It could be more involved: **Hee, sirimasen desita.** or **Yappari soo desu ka.** It could also be a comment: **Sore zyaa, komatta desyoo nee.** Note that the last example can function both as a comment to a previous answer and a way to elicit further information about the situation being discussed.

   – Use sentences other than interrogative sentences to elicit information. You can use many of the conversational reaction utterances for this purpose. You can also suggest a continuation by the other speaker, using phrases such as **Soo desu ka. Zyaa..** or **Miraa-san o sagasite iru n desu ga..**

   – To the extent possible, give a larger authentic context in which it would be natural for the teacher to be posing questions. A common reason for intensive questioning in a language classroom is to check on students' comprehension. By introducing other, less classroom-like contexts, you can avoid a mode of interaction that occurs only in an instructional setting. For example, you might be a supervisor in an office who wants to hear about a conversation that took place between your subordinate worker and a client. Setting such a context will make the content questioning an authentic communicative activity and make it easier to ask questions in a manner less like interrogation.

Depending on the CC, content questioning may follow initial CC practice but precede contextualized performance. This order is particularly useful when the CC is relatively long and complex. Through questioning on the content, the forms that have been practiced may be reinforced to help lead to a smooth performance. You can make certain that students have a clear understanding of the content before they perform the conversation in context, which in turn will raise their confidence level.

EXTENDED DISCOURSE EXERCISES

Effective situational exercises make full use of rehearsed elements but place them in a larger communicative context. CC performance activities, especially CC expansion and CC variation, constitute one type of situational exercise. In these exercises, learners must consider the context of interaction to be able to select and perform a certain CC at a given moment with appropriate expansions and variations. At the same time, learners also rely on the predetermined discourse structure of the CC. Exchanges rehearsed in Drill practice may also be expanded, combined, and varied to develop an extended discourse. Application Exercises included at the end of Sections A and B of each lesson in the textbook provide useful suggestions for situational exercises. To use them, set up a number of sequenced mini-contexts to guide students in an extended discourse. The following hints are useful for planning and implementing situational extended discourse exercises.

- Devise the presentation of contexts to elicit the target behavior from students without modeling it. All Drills in *JSL-MC* are response drills in which learners practice respond-ing to a context presented orally by another person. While this kind of practice is different from the imitation practice used for CCs, learners are given an exact model of the kind of linguistic manipulation they must perform to produce correct Drill responses. The response is not pre-determined in a context-ualized discourse exercise, but the context you establish must be sufficiently clear for students to understand, and it must be one for which they can provide an appropriate response from their repertoire of Japanese.

- Make sure that the elicited language and behavior are culturally appropriate. Extensive practice of wrong forms is counterproductive.

- Design activities so that students engage in authen-tic tasks of communication. Make certain that the interactions are likely to occur in the target culture and are not simply linguistic translations of what would occur only in the students' native culture.

- The communicative tasks should involve practice of the new patterns introduced in the given lesson, and these forms should be used by the students, not just the instructors. To increase student partici-pation, determine the target items that students need to practice, then think of a context that will enable students to use them. Finally, consider additional expressions, especially review items, that may be practiced in the same context. Develop the exercise as needed to incorporate the full range of possible expressions.

- When you suggest a modification, give students the opportunity to use the modification in an interaction. Have them repeat the modified form, and then have them use the modified form in a communicative situation. These two steps are time consuming but crucially important, for they enable the learner to successfully perform Japanese in Japanese cultural contexts.

MODIFICATIONS THROUGH ERROR CORRECTION DURING REHEARSED ACTIVITIES

Even with the extensive practicing and self-monitoring made possible by *JSL-MC*, students are likely to need some guidance to correct some of their behavior. The goal of correction during performance practice is to enable students to successfully engage in Japanese interaction without constantly being concerned about the accuracy of their linguistic forms or their body language. Successful interaction is free of language that invites misunderstanding, impedes comprehension, or causes discomfort on the part of one's interaction partner. Beginning learners of Japanese are required to learn a very different system of interaction from that of American culture, so they are likely to need special coaching. Note the following general points about correction during communicative activities.

- Do not frighten, intimidate, or browbeat students with correction. Learning does not take place in such an atmosphere; instead, the student simply tries to please the teacher in an attitude of desperation. If correction has to become the center of classroom activity, perhaps the activity is too difficult for the learners.

- Give feedback without exaggeration. Positive feedback is just as important as negative feedback, but avoid exaggerated praise. A quick nod of approval may be all that is needed. In any normal conversational situation, successful use of the language is met not with repeated praise but with smooth continuing interaction.

- Give students the opportunity for self-correction. The ability to correct is an important indication of learning. You may simply ask for a repetition or, if needed, indicate that there was some communicative problem as you request the repetition. When possible, use a natural conversational prompt for repetition. For example, rather than **moo iti-do itte kudasai**, which is typical classroom dialect, use **E?/Hai?, Sumimasen. Nan desu ka./**. Sometimes just a puzzled look can trigger a student's repetition with self-correction. Peer correction may be encouraged to some extent, but can encourage students to depend on help from classmates. What is more, while some students find peer correction to be less stressful than being corrected by a teacher, many students resent correction by peers.

- Always be prepared to provide a model. Remember that no type of correction will work if students have not learned the forms they need for what they are trying to express. However, systematic errors (e.g., pronouncing all **ko-so-a-do** words with an accent on the first mora) always require prompt correction by the teacher.

- Provide only a correct model. Do not try to imitate a learner's error. From the learner's point of view, it may not be clear whether you are imitating the error or providing a correct model, thus leading to confusion and frustration. Imagine the result when a learner imitates an instructor's imitation of incorrect Japanese. Learners should be able to assume that the Japanese you use is always a correct model.

- If necessary, slow down slightly for model presentation, but be sure to stay within the range of natural speech. If you do slow down, go back to a more normal conversational speed before students begin their imitation. Similarly, if you use special emphasis to make a point, return to speech without any special emphasis before students begin to imitate you.

- Do not focus on a single student for an extended period of time. Doing so becomes boring for everyone else and embarrassing for the one student who is being repeatedly corrected. Instead, offer correction twice to the student who needs it, then give several other students quick model-repetition practice on the same item (during which the student having a problem has time to observe and analyze the difficulty). Finally, give the original student an opportunity to provide a corrected repetition. These three steps may require one more repetition, but more than that will probably prove fruitless. In such cases, the teacher should make a mental note of the difficulty and the student for future drill.

- Always return to the interactive situation. A student's ability to repeat a correct form does not guarantee competence to use it correctly in a communicative situation.

- The timing of correction is important. The longer the period of time between the occurrence of an error and the correction of it, the less impact the correction will have. Constant interruptive corrections, however, hinder the flow of an interactive discourse. In general, let students complete an entire script-based conversation like the performance of a CC before making corrections. Make note of any body language errors or linguistic mistakes or problems with the overall flow of discourse, and then correct them after the CC performance. Once problem areas have been pointed out and practiced, recurring errors in subsequent performances of the same CC should be pointed out immediately to encourage learners' self-correction ability.

SECTION 3:
DISCUSSION SESSIONS: LANGUAGE LEARNING, CULTURE, AND LANGUAGE

Adequate student preparation outside of class enables you to spend the greater part of class time using the Japanese language, but occasional discussions using English can benefit student progress in Japanese. This chapter considers three areas in which English discussion sessions may be useful: language learning, Japanese culture, and Japanese language in cultural contexts. For discussion of language learning, use the *User's Guide* for reference. As a basis for further discussions of Japanese culture, use the CC video or the CD-ROM program as well as the culture video selections. The textbook, *A Question and Answer Supplement*, and the CD-ROM program are useful resources for a discussion of language and of some features of behavioral culture.

OBJECTIVES

We gain competence in our native language during a lifetime of socialization. By the time we enter school and begin to talk *about* our language and behavior, we are already able to use the language for oral communication and, to some extent, for written communication as well. Schooling and additional socialization refine our linguistic ability for a greater number of purposes and in a greater number of registers. Adult foreign learners of Japanese do not have the luxury of time available to children acquiring their native language. Cognitively, however, mature learners are able to analyze their experiences and learn from analyses presented to them. The primary objective of discussion sessions conducted in English is to provide information about the learning process and the target of learning so as to maximize the efficiency of the learning process.

In some language programs, the instructional staff includes both a teacher (or teachers) whose primary function is to talk *about* Japanese (a "fact" teacher) and a teacher (or teachers) whose primary function is to help students *perform* in Japanese (an "act" teacher). In such cases, most of the discussion sessions described next are best led by the "fact" teacher. If there is only one teacher, the time during which English is used for communication is best limited and kept separate from the time when Japanese is practiced and used for communication. It is only these latter hours that actually produce an ability to speak and understand a foreign language.

Discussion about Language Learning

Novice learners of Japanese enter a classroom with a set of assumptions about learning. Some of these assumptions are useful in learning spoken Japanese, while others may slow down progress. You can orient your students by providing clear goals for the program of instruction and by promoting learning strategies that will help them in their studies.

Program Goals and Course Objectives

Whatever the subject matter, a well-designed program of instruction has a clearly defined set of program goals. Courses within that program will contribute collectively to those program goals. Thus, the objectives of a course such as Japanese 101 are determined by the goals of the program within which it exists. *JSL-MC* is a useful set of learning materials for introductory courses in a program that has as one of its goals culturally appropriate oral interaction with Japanese in Japanese.

Inform your students of the course objectives and the program goals and explain how the learning materials contribute to those goals. Describe the goals in terms of what learners will be able to do as a result of taking the course. If *JSL-MC* is used alone in the course, explain the concentration on the spoken language. If it is used in combination with materials that introduce the written language, explain how the two types of materials will be used. (See the *User's Guide* for a fuller discussion of this subject.) If one or two components of *JSL-MC* are to supplement other learning material, spell out how the main material and supplementary material differ in the way students are to use them. In all cases, be sure that students understand what they are expected to do outside of class as preparation and what they can expect to experience in class based on their preparation.

Learning Strategies

JSL-MC, and especially the design of the CD-ROM program, fosters strategies that will be helpful to students for learning oral communication while guiding them away from unproductive strategies. The following are some examples of the features of *JSL-MC* that encourage learners to use cognitive, metacognitive, and socioaffective strategies for effective learning.

- The CD-ROM program directs the learner's attention to the representation of Japanese sounds. Because the aim of *JSL-MC* is to help learners master spoken Japanese, they encounter new linguistic forms through sounds with visual images of the contexts in which corresponding interactions occur.

- *JSL-MC* fosters self-monitoring and self-evaluation by learners. All practice sessions provide audiorecordings and instant replay functions. Learners can compare their speech samples with models and monitor themselves for improvement on their own. Listening comprehension and production can also be verified and corrected by learners on their own.

- Learners are constantly reminded of the larger cultural framework within which language becomes meaningful. The cognitive capacity of learners is expanded beyond the linguistic code, enabling them to continue their learning as they use a steadily growing body of knowledge of the cultural framework of the language.

- Systematic explanations of facts about the language support extensive practice activities designed to develop procedural skills. Together, they encourage a balance between inductive and deductive learning.

- New information about the language and new skills used in the language build on what has already been learned, allowing learners to be creative while not breaking the social and linguistic rules of language use.

- Learners are encouraged to ask questions about linguistic forms and their underlying cultural system.

- Information about Japanese society and culture is integrated with language learning in support of practice in contextualized language use.

- At various points in the program, learners have the opportunity to measure their progress. Such concrete measurements provide continuous motivation for further study.

- One's ability to participate in spoken interaction demonstrates one's level of competence in the spoken language. The anxiety that may arise from having to perform can be reduced by providing the learner with an organized, appropriately paced course for practice in the skills needed for such performance.

Mention these strategies overtly not only at the beginning of the program, but throughout the program.

CULTURE IN THE LANGUAGE PROGRAM

Culture is a highly complex concept. A given culture shapes the way its members act, interact, and think, but their acting and thinking shape the culture as well. Culture, therefore, exists in a constant cycle of self-generation, making it extremely difficult to define exactly what constitutes a culture. When we use the phrase "Japanese culture," we refer both to the way a Japanese individual views the world and to the collective knowledge the people of Japan possess. The difficulty of examining a foreign culture lies in this double nature of culture. Culture is a very different entity depending on who views it, when, and under what circumstances. For this reason, Hector Hammerly proposes a three-way categorization of culture: achievement culture, informational culture, and behavioral culture.[2]

Achievement culture refers to ways of expression achieved through a set of skills attained consciously over a period of time. These ways of expression are thought to charac-terize a given culture and, typically, include such aspects as literature, music, dance, traditional cuisine, fashion, and painting. Being a native of Japan does not in itself enable a person to be a performer of Japanese dance: Such a skill requires extensive training for anyone, native or nonnative, who wishes to engage in it.

Informational culture refers to the kind of information that people who are socialized in the culture normally are taught and know. The names of the prefectures of Japan are an example of informational culture. The names of major Japanese literary works and political parties as well as knowledge about historical events and economic poli-cies are also learned through study and socialization.

Behavioral culture refers to the way members of a culture behave, with or without conscious effort. For example, people who grow up in Japan bow in certain situations without awareness of their actions. Only when the bow is missing do they develop awareness of it. This kind of culture is most tightly interwoven with language. In fact, language may be considered a manifestation of behavioral culture: Learning behavioral culture is an integral part of learning a language.

Culture, especially behavioral and informational culture, is an integral component of *JSL-MC*. Every activity in the audiotapes, textbook, *A Question and Answer Supplement*, and the CD-ROM program takes

---

[2] *Synthesis in Second Language Teaching: An Introduction to Linguistics* (Blaine, WA: Second Language Publications [1982]), 513–514.

behavioral culture into consideration. As a basis for discussion of contrasts with behavioral culture in English, use the CC video. For discussions of Japanese informational culture, use the selection of eight culture videos.

DISCUSSING BEHAVIORAL CULTURE USING CC VIDEO SEGMENTS

Use the CD-ROM program, if available, or the CC video to observe and discuss each CC—both the action and the setting—before students practice it. To the extent the students' ability in Japanese permits, carry out these discussions in Japanese.

Silent Viewing of a CC

Play the video segment of the desired CC first without sound. Play it as many times as needed to permit careful observation. On the CD-ROM program, the video controller located at the bottom of the video screen allows you to adjust the sound and to play any segment of the CC video with a simple maneuvering of the mouse. To lower the volume, quickly click on the pause button on the video controller, hold down the speaker button to adjust the volume, then resume play by clicking on the play button. Questions you might ask about the video include:

- Who are the speakers? What kind of predicate forms do you expect? For example, Mr. Carter and Mr. Suzuki, colleagues at a bank, have been using formal (distal) predicates but not many polite forms in conversing with each other. If you are using the CD-ROM program, go to the Who's Who section by way of the Main Menu to review the relationships among the characters portrayed in the CC video.

- Where is this conversation taking place, and what are the speakers doing? Given the setting, what are they likely to be talking about? For example, if the conversation appears to take place during an office coffee break, the speakers might be engaged in small talk or they might be talking shop. You can confirm the topic of conversation by selecting the Setting button in the CD-ROM program or going through the Miscellaneous Notes in the textbook.

- What is the physical distance between the speakers? How significant is it? For example, the desk at which Mr. Yamada sits is extremely close to that of Ms. Miller. Office space seems very limited, with little privacy for individual workers. Is this generally true in Japan?

- What body language do you observe? Note, for example, bowing, hand positions and movements, eye contact, facial expressions, and the speed of movements.

- What kind of clothes are the speakers wearing? What does this say about the setting and the conversational partners? For example, what does it mean when the two men are both wearing suits, but only the older man is wearing a vest as well? Does the vest imply perhaps that the older person is a senior employee?

Viewing the CC with Sound

Show the video segment again, this time with sound. Students can now confirm and correct some of the hypotheses made during the silent viewing of the video. You can make a few additional observations, such as:

- What is the relative speed of speech of each speaker?

- With what kind of timing do speakers take turns speaking? For example, one speaker may interject **hai** and **soo desu ka.**, almost overlapping the speech of the other.

- What is the coordination of gestures with language, for example, between bowing and verbal apology or between hand movements and a negative statement?

- What kinds of predicates and sentence particles do the speakers use? For example, do the speakers use -**desu** / -**masu** forms and sentence particles **yo** and **nee**, and if so, what do these signify?

- To what extent can you tell what the conversation is about?

After the first lesson of *JSL*, much of the content of a CC in the next lesson will be familiar to the learner; only a limited number of new vocabulary items and structural patterns will be introduced in each subsequent lesson.

DISCUSSING INFORMATIONAL CULTURE USING CULTURE VIDEOS

Culture videos in a language program are useful for providing information on the development of some features of behavior observed in modern Japan. Basic information about Japan, its educational system, history, economy, and cultural achievements gives learners an incentive to participate in Japanese culture themselves. More important, it allows language learners to share part of the knowledge base that the members of Japanese society assume, and helps in students' communication with the Japanese.

Of the eight culture videos selected for inclusion in *JSL-MC*, the three video selections from the *Pacific Century* series present extensive archival materials covering the period from the late nineteenth century to the late twentieth century, with clear explanations in English by eminent historians and witnesses to major historical events. The videos present historical perspectives on the changes Japan has undergone. The first change was the opening of the country to Western culture and the resulting industrialization after about 200 years of almost total isolation; the second change came about as a result of Japan's defeat in World War II; and the third was Japan's self-regulated transformation into an international economic superpower. The commentaries provided by historians as well as people who experienced key events in Japan's recent history are woven together with numerous photographs, drawings, and video footage to illustrate the historical background of today's Japan.

The five-video series *Faces of Japan II* is a collection of 15-minute video segments that portray representatives of contemporary Japanese society, including one non-Japanese living in Japan. These videos invite learners of the Japanese language to visit diverse segments of Japanese society. The videos, which have their own teacher's guide, are suitable for study with students in grades 7 through 12.

For procedures for using the culture videos in class, see Section 6.

DISCUSSING LANGUAGE FORMS IN CULTURAL CONTEXTS

The textbook, *A Question and Answer Supplement*, and the CD-ROM program use examples to explain linguistic forms and the cultural system that underlies them. The audiotapes contain English explanations covering the setting of each CC and each set of Drill exchanges. The textbook and the CD-ROM program also contain information about the contexts of the CCs and the language used in them. If students are able to take advantage of all these multimedia tools outside of class, only a small portion of class time will be needed to review the most important points and complex concepts. Otherwise, it will be necessary to spend class time going over these explanations and descriptions. In either case, let students assume responsibility for outside study and learning from as many of these multimedia tools as are available to them. They should then ask questions only when they need help. Avoid the temptation to give lectures on everything you feel is important, which would essentially repeat what is in these materials.

To be able to ask meaningful questions about particular features of a language, students first must have encountered examples of those features. There is no question that explanations have a greater impact if students are already familiar with what is being explained. This order is implicit in the textbook and even more so in the CD-ROM program, which plays the CC video automatically each time a CC is selected. Students are expected to view the video and listen to the conversation several times before they read about the setting or newly introduced structural patterns.

CC Translation (Optional)

After students have had a chance to see and hear the video segment of a CC, discuss the content of the conversation by selecting the Translation button in the CD-ROM program or looking at the English Equivalent in the textbook. Some of the hypotheses made during the initial viewing of the video will be confirmed or modified.

- Show the translation of the entire CC to students and give them a chance to ask questions about the content of the conversation. Point out features of the CC language and setting that are especially typical of Japan.

- If you are using the CD-ROM program, click on each unit of translation (i.e., a single turn in the conversation) to have students listen to the corresponding segment of the conversation in Japanese. Note that the translation disappears while the corresponding portion of the Japanese conversation is playing, encouraging the students to pay attention to the video segment.

- Have students identify expressions that are new to them.

CC Notes and Transcription

- If you are using the CD-ROM program in class, show the list of items in the Notes section; otherwise, have students read the Miscellaneous Notes in the textbook. For each item listed, have students comment on any observation they may have made before reading the notes.

- Give students an opportunity to ask further questions about the items, but don't get involved in explanations that are too advanced for the students to handle at the moment.

- Show the students the transcription, either by clicking on the Transcription button in the CD-ROM program or turning to the CC presentation section of the textbook.

- On the CD-ROM program screen, click on each of the transcription boxes to play one portion of the conversation at a time. Note that the transcription disappears during the corresponding portion of the Japanese conversation, encouraging the students to pay attention to the video segment.

Structural Patterns

Use the CD-ROM program, if available, as well as *A Question and Answer Supplement* and the textbook as the basis for discussion. Start by going over the CCs in the particular section.

- Ask students if they have questions about any of the forms introduced in the set of CCs in the given section.

- Depending on the questions students ask, select the relevant sections in the CD-ROM program or in *A Question and Answer Supplement*.

- Point out the portions of the Structural Patterns (SPs) for students to review.

In addition to questions about the occurrence of specific forms in the CCs, students may need help in understanding some of the Drill exchanges (CD-ROM program and audiotapes), Eavesdropping selections

(CD-ROM program and audiotapes), Utilization samples (CD-ROM program), Check-up questions (textbook), or Structure Check questions (CD-ROM program). Reserve a set amount of time to handle these problems.

Once learners have gained an understanding of the linguistic forms and the cultural system, they are ready to engage in basic practice to develop skills in using the language, as outlined in the next chapter.

SECTION 4:
REHEARSING IN CLASS WITH MULTIMEDIA TOOLS

This chapter presents examples of basic practice activities. It describes procedures for using *JSL-MC* in class in ways not used by individual students outside of class. The CD-ROM program, audiotapes, and CC videotape of *JSL-MC* may be used for this purpose in a multimedia classroom in which each student has individual access to the program or in a classroom where the instructor controls the program or tape.

OBJECTIVES

Being able to manipulate linguistic forms is a necessary skill for successful communication but is not in itself the final goal of learning a foreign language. Many learners, and even some teachers, consider basic practice to be a tedious step that they would avoid if they could. However, it can be highly rewarding when learners experience, in a concrete way, improvements in their competence by using these skills in task-oriented communicative situations as outlined in Section 2.

There are three advantages to doing basic practice in class.

- It enables you to monitor the students' performance at this basic level of learning. Whether an expert learner or a native speaker, a trained instructor can help students judge whether they are ready to proceed to the next activity or should review further. This kind of help is especially important at the beginning. Eventually, and certainly before they leave an instructional program, learners should have the ability to manage their own learning.

- The prompt and appropriate advice you provide students during the basic practice phase will reduce their random guesswork and will make the learning experience more efficient. You may make suggestions about correction or decide that learners are within an acceptable range of variation, depending on the nature and the degree of deviation from the model in their speech. Feedback during basic practice promotes the necessary confidence for students to apply basic skills in communicative situations.

• You can combine basic practice with more communicative activities in class, as outlined in Section 2. Plan your class hour so that students have the opportunity to use their linguistic skills and knowledge to accomplish interactional tasks. Be flexible, providing students with adequate time for basic practice, but always be prepared to engage them in contextualized activities as soon as they are ready.

CC Vocabulary and Build-up Practice with the CD-ROM Program or Audiotapes

If your students practice the CCs with audiotapes or with the CD-ROM program before coming to class, skip this section and move on to Role Play. For in-class practice of CCs, also review the basic procedures outlined in the *User's Guide*.

Both Vocabulary and Build-up Practice involve imitating a model.

• Have students listen to the model and repeat it. Repeat this step as many times as is needed. In a large class, this may be done once or twice in chorus format, but students should have an opportunity for individual performance as well. Spend more time on difficult items.

• Work on pronunciation problems by isolating the problem areas.

– For example, students often mispronounce the final portion of sentences ending in -su plus particle yo (e.g., **Ii desu yo**) as -syoo (**Ii desyoo**). In this particular example, isolating **ii desu** will not help, since the vowel in utterance-final -su is typically devoiced. Isolate the /**su yo**/ portion from this example, saying it carefully a few times, then immediately provide the entire example, **Ii desu yo**, as a model for imitation. Students can now be expected to pay more careful attention to the pronunciation of /**su yo**/ within it, but ensure that they practice saying only meaningful sequences.

– For correcting errors in pitch accent and intonation, it sometimes helps to show a contour with a hand movement. Be sure that the contour matches what you are saying. If you are facing the students, move your hand from right to left to enable them to see your hand move from left to right.

For example, the word **kore** presents an accent problem for many native speakers of English. In addition, when it is used within a question sentence, the English question intonation is often incorrectly substituted for the Japanese. Thus, students are apt to say either *****Kôre desu ka./** (wrong accent placement) or *****Kore desu ka?** (Wrong intonation) rather than the correct **Koré dèsu ka./** To signal the correct accent and intonation patterns, say this sentence while moving your hand as shown in Figure 4-1.

Figure 4-1
Hand Movements to Illustrate Accent and Intonation

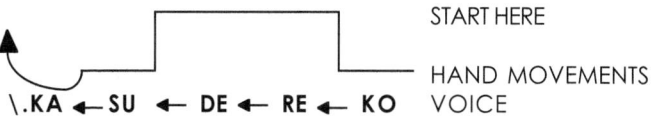

		START HERE
\.KA ← SU ← DE ← RE ← KO		HAND MOVEMENTS
		VOICE

CC Role Play with the CD-ROM Program or CC Video

(At this point, also review the basic procedures outlined in the *User's Guide*.)

• Assign each of the speaker's roles in the CC to one of a pair of students.

• Play the CC video silently, having pairs of students provide the sound as they watch the video. If your class is large, divide it in half, assigning one role to each group. Now have the two groups practice the CC along with the video. After doing this once or twice, have a few pairs of individual students practice the role play.

• If students have trouble performing the CC smoothly, return to the Vocabulary or Build-up section and work on the segments that require further practice.

• Proceed with the substitution, expansion, and variation activities outlined in Section 2.

Drills with the CD-ROM Program

Use the basic procedures outlined in the *User's Guide* to practice the Drills in the CD-ROM program in class. When the Drill exchange involves manipulation of specific objects (e.g., giving, receiving, or showing items), bring these objects to the classroom. Try to vary and expand on the exchanges when possible and useful.

• Select the desired Drill from the Drill Menu.

• After the two model exchanges, ensure that students have grasped the specific pattern they are required to use in their responses. If necessary, replay the models.

- If your class is held in a multimedia classroom with a terminal for each student, students can record their own responses. Otherwise, have one student provide the response in each exchange. Repeat this through several exchanges of the Drill.

- When students are able to respond to the cues smoothly, have pairs of students exchange utterances with each other, using the pattern of the Drill and manipulating the props and visual aids as appropriate. For example, Drill A in Lesson 4B involves requesting a certain number of objects:

(Cue)	(Response)
Kono nooto wa?	**Ni-satu kudasai.**
Kono pen wa?	**Ni-hon kudasai.**

- Take objects to class, e.g., notebooks, pens, *furoshiki*, books, and pencils, and have the students act out the Drill exchanges with appro-priate accompanying activities.

- Encourage self-correction, but if students are unable to detect their errors or to correct them on their own, provide help. The acceptability of content and form of the response needs to be checked as well as structure and pronunciation. When a student who has been corrected is able to imitate the model response satisfactorily, go back to the interactional mode and require a corrected response to the cue. Repeating and responding involve very different mental tasks.

- After practicing the Drills in their original form, vary elements of the exchanges as appropriate. In the example above (Lesson 4B, Drill A), the quantity of each item requested in the responses is always *two*. Now vary the number of items asked for and manipulate the props accordingly, making the

practice more complex as well as more spontaneous.

- Expand the selection. Practice the Drill pattern
further, using items that are not included in the
Drill. In the previous example, add silverware,
paper plates, pamphlets, and other items with
which to practice familiar classifiers in similar
exchanges. Note that students will now use **kore**
rather than **kono X** in their cues, since they do not
yet know how to name these objects in Japanese.

- Expand the exchanges. Almost all examples in the
Drills in *JSL 1* involve only two turns—one cue
and one response. The result is often only a small
portion of what would be a more complete interaction. Thus the Drill exchanges can be embedded
in longer contexts. For example, Drill F in Lesson
5A involves exchanges that might take place
between a customer and a sales clerk:

(Cue)   (Response)

Kaban wa, kore dake   **Kaban desu ka./ Iie,**
desu ka./   **kaban wa, takusan**
                               arimasu kedo..

In an actual store, the conversation would
probably continue. You can play the role of the
customer and bring the shopping scene to a likely
closure as follows:

(Cue)	(Response)
Kaban wa, kore dake desu ka./	**Kaban desu ka./ Iie, takusan arimasu kedo..**
Soo desu ka. Motto ookii no mo arimasu ka./	**Gozaimasu yo./ Kore desu kedo..**
A, zyaa kore kudasai.	**Maido arigatoo gozaimasu.**

Note that in this expanded version, the student will have the added opportunity to listen to a new pattern (**motto ookii no**) and a new vocabulary item (**gozaimasu**) that were introduced in this lesson, with the resulting conversation an application of the CCs of this lesson.

UTILIZATION WITH THE CD-ROM PROGRAM

Utilization is a simulated interactional exercise. It is different from the communicative activities discussed in Section 2 in that the circumstances of the interaction are presented in English. However, it is not a translation exercise; students perform tasks according to a description but do *not* translate that description. It is helpful for you to bring appropriate props to class to reinforce the various contexts, but Utilization does not require you to develop those contexts to elicit students' utterances.

- To prepare for Utilization in class, review the Models and the Models in Context as provided in the CD-ROM program. Make note of other possible appropriate utterances. Prepare any props you want to use for reinforcement.

- Show the English description of the situation. Check to ensure that students have understood the situation clearly—in addition to the description of the situation, the CD-ROM program directs learners either to respond to another speaker or to begin the conversation.

- Use props as appropriate. For example, consider Lesson 1, Utilization #21: "A comment has been made about how often you go to the movies. Agree with reservation." For this Utilization, it would be useful to have several flyers advertising movies.

- If the student is to respond, initiate the conversation or direct another student to do so. A possible way to initiate a conversation in the above example would be:

(Teacher) [pointing to the movie flyers]

Yoku ikimasu nee.

(Student)

Ee, maa.

If the student is to initiate the conversation, the response should be provided by you or another student. Consider another example from Lesson 1 (#22): "A sweater you have had made is too big. Find out if it can be made small[er]." For this, the teacher may assign another student (S2) to play the role of the second speaker, who made the sweater. The following conversation might then occur:

(S1) **Sumimasen. Tyotto, tiisaku dekimasen ka./**

(S2) **Dekimasu yo!**

Of course, S2 has the option of responding with **Tyotto..**, indicating a problem in complying.

- If the designated student is unable to take part in the exchange, ask another student to try. If the second student also fails, click on the Model button and let the students try again after they have heard the model.

- Compare the exchange with the model in Context. Discuss any differences between each student's speech sample and the model provided in the CD-ROM program.

- Expand on the conversation, stretching the students as much as possible within their capabilities, but being careful not to require performance beyond their competence level. The preceding example, including the alternative response, might be:

(S1) **Sumimasen. Tyotto, tiisaku dekimasen ka./**

(S2) **Tyotto..**

(S1) **Dekimasen ka./**

(S2) **Sumimasen.** (or **Moosiwake arimasen.**)

Note that this expansion gives additional opportunity for the contextualized practice of negative questions, one of the key structures in this lesson.

Utilization is very different from the performance of a CC. It provides students with the opportunity to synthesize what they have learned and apply it in new contexts. These exchanges should be expanded to practice longer discourse, but they should not be used as the basis for CC substitution or variation activities.

SECTION 5:
ASSESSMENT STRATEGIES: TASKS AND PROCEDURES

Whether or not students use the program extensively outside of class, the different components of *JSL-MC* can be used in class for assessment purposes. This usage is particularly helpful if the teacher's proficiency level is limited. This chapter describes the ways of using the multimedia tools to assess student learning of basic discourse (CCs), linguistic forms (Drills and SPs), comprehension (Eavesdropping), and applied production (Utilization). It also suggests ways of constructing meaningful interview tests.

Many of the activities outlined here are similar to the rehearsed activities described in Section 2; in fact, you can assess student preparation to a large degree by engaging in these performance activities. It is important not to correct student errors during assessment activities, but it is equally important to offer students feedback and correction soon after the assessment phase.

REHEARSED ORAL INTERACTION (CC CHECK)

To check students' preparation of a CC, use the CD-ROM program or audiotape and follow these steps:

1. Have the first few students act out the CC, using the procedures of the Role Play practice on the CD-ROM program or the audiotape. Have the remaining students perform the CC with pairs of students taking each role so that you can move through the check more quickly but still detect individual errors. This activity tests whether students have practiced the CC enough to be able to perform it smoothly.

2. If there are supplementary vocabulary items associated with the CC, incorporate them during the second round of CC performances or, if the class is large, after several pairs have performed the CC in its original

form. This activity tests whether students know the CC well enough to manipulate it with simple substitutions.

After all students have performed the CC once, with or without the substitution of supplementary vocabulary, engage in additional practice, this time with correction. When students can take part in the CC freely, with only few, if any, minor errors, proceed to application exercises, including expansion and variation practice, as outlined in Section 2.

STRUCTURE (DRILLS, SPS, STRUCTURE CHECK)

To see whether students are able to manipulate linguistic forms smoothly, use the Drills in the CD-ROM program or the audiotapes. To check students' understanding of the structures, use the SP section of the CD-ROM program, questions from *A Question and Answer Supplement*, or the Check-up section in the textbook.

Drill Check (the CD-ROM Program or Audiotapes)

Use the following procedures to determine whether students have mastered the Drills. For this check, the CD-ROM program is much easier to use than the audiotapes. As audiotapes are cumbersome, you may find it easier to provide the cue sentences yourself, bypassing the tapes entirely.

1. Select one of the assigned Drills and have students take turns responding to the cues. This activity tests the level of automaticity with which students are able to manipulate the forms.

2. Use additional visual aids to practice the same pattern in different contexts. Expand on each exchange when appropriate and possible. This activity tests whether students are able to manipulate the forms automatically while comprehending the meaning of each exchange.

Follow the assessment phase with additional practice that includes correction. When students are able to respond to cues quickly and accurately, move on to a more contextualized exercise.

Structural Pattern Questioning (the CD-ROM Program or *A Question and Answer Supplement*)

By separately assessing student understanding of structural aspects of Japanese and comparing the results with the results of oral assessment, you can identify the nature of problems that students are having. Do the problems arise from a lack of structural understanding, or do they stem from a lack of practice? Once you isolate the source, you can give students appropriate guidance.

1. Select an SP from the SP Menu.

2. Have the students read the question silently. Call on one student for an answer.

3. If using the CD-ROM program, check the answer by selecting the Answer button. Discuss any differences between that answer and the student's answer.

4. If appropriate, elicit examples of the pattern from students.

5. If using the CD-ROM program, click on the Example button and study the examples given in the program.

As an alternative, you can have students write their answers to selected questions. Once their papers are collected, go over the questions, this time showing the model answers for each question. You may also use selected questions from *A Question and Answer Supplement* or the Check-up section of the textbook as part of a quiz. However, some of the Check-up questions in the textbook require answers that are too long for a short quiz.

Structure Check with the CD-ROM Program

Once students have practiced the CCs and Drills extensively and have gone over the SP questions, use the multiple-choice Structure Check questions in Section C of each lesson in the CD-ROM program to assess the students' understanding of the important structural and sociolinguistic features of the Japanese introduced in that lesson. Because the correct answer to each question in the Structure Check is always indicated before the next question is given, have students work in pairs and have them check each other's answers. It is best to use a single monitor and for the teacher to control the time spent on each question.

1. Open the first question in the Structure Check section.

2. Once students have had time to read the first question and mark their answer, they will show it to their partners.

3. Have the two students in each pair check each other's answer and mark the answer sheet before going on to the next question.

4. When all questions have been answered and the answers checked by student partners, collect the answer sheets.

5. As soon as you collect the answer sheets, go over those questions that caused the most difficulty.

COMPREHENSION

In programs in which students study using the CD-ROM program or the audiotapes outside of class, assign Eavesdropping as homework. The CD-ROM program offers immediate feedback so that students can monitor their listening comprehension ability.

You may also use the Eavesdropping section of the CD-ROM program in class for assessment of listening comprehension. When Eavesdropping exercises are assigned as homework, students are able to listen to the Japanese selections repeatedly, but when they are used for testing, students are allowed to listen to the selections only once. To give equal listening opportunity to all students during class, use a single monitor for the entire group and go through the following procedures:

1. Go to the first selection in the Eavesdropping Menu in Section C. The Japanese selection will play once automatically.

2. Have students write on pieces of paper their answers to the questions for the selection without showing them the answers.

3. Repeat steps 1 and 2 for all of the selections you have chosen for assessment.

4. Collect answer sheets from the students.

5. Go back to the selections and review all of the answers. This time, check the model answers and, if necessary, replay the selections and discuss the answers.

You may also use the audiotapes for assessment, but doing so will require more planning. Before playing the tape in class, you must go through it in advance to mark the counter numbers corresponding to the location of each selection you want to use for the assessment. Alternatively, you can act out the selected exchanges in front of the students or, preferably, invite another competent speaker of Japanese to class to act out the exchanges with you.

SIMULATION USING UTILIZATION

To check students' performance in Utilization for pur-poses of assessment, follow the Utilization procedures outlined in Section 4 but give each student his or her performance grade. Never permit students to write their answers, because Utilization is a simulated oral exercise, not translation or writing practice. If you assign Utilization as homework, you should either spend class time checking the students' oral performance or have them record their answers on audiotapes to be handed in.

MONITORING STUDENT LEARNING

One of the special features of the CD-ROM program is its Record Session Information function. This function enables you to monitor what your students do during their learning sessions and to collect useful data on student learning behavior for research purposes or for advising.

Activating the Record Session Information Function

See the "Getting Started" section of the *User's Guide* on how to activate this function and to access the recorded data. In assigning students designations, it may be helpful to give all students in the same class the same session name. Session names might be something like "11/6B," in which *11/6* designates a date and *B* indicates a particular group of students or a class.

Type of Data Recorded

The Record Session Information function records log-in time and the time when various function and navigation buttons are clicked. The recorded data are stored as simple text on the hard drive of the computer or on a separate diskette, if provided. Students' answers for Eavesdropping, Utilization, and Structure Check are not kept by the program. To gather data on the Utilization exercises, you will need to have a separate voice recorder at each student's workstation.

THE ORAL INTERVIEW

The assessment activities discussed thus far primarily measure the extent to which students have learned the information and skills associated with discrete portions of the various components of *JSL-MC*. To measure general ability to use spoken Japanese for meaningful participation in Japanese contextual interactions, you will need to design an oral interview. To a large extent, an oral interview will resemble a CC application or the extended discourse practice outlined in Section 2. However, an oral interview should be more comprehensive in content. It requires scripting a conversation, performing the conversation, and providing feedback to the student.

Scripting an Oral Interview

To use the oral interview as an assessment tool in an instructional program, you must give the same interview to all students being tested.

Decide whether the oral interview test is to be a proficiency test or an achievement test. If it is to measure the general ability of the students to perform in Japanese, regardless of what has been specifically presented and practiced in the instructional program, it is a proficiency test. If it is to measure the ability of the student to use what was presented and practiced in interactional settings during the program, it is an achievement test. For both types of tests, you will first need to develop a detailed conversational script. The following discussion assumes that the oral interview is being used for achievement testing.[3]

1. After determining what you expect the student to say during the conversation, make sure that the student's repertoire includes the appropriate patterns and vocabulary. Remember that if the interviewer uses a wide range of material but the student gets by with short answers, the interview is of limited value.

---

[3] This type of testing, i.e., an achievement test in a proficiency format, is known as prochievement testing.

2. Organize the interview so that students have a frequent chance to use newly learned forms. Without providing such a measure, each oral interview can last for a long time without demonstrating a student's true competence, making it impossible to use the interview as an integral part of the curriculum, especially when one teacher must interview many students.

3. Expect variation among students. Do not make the script dependent on a specific or unique student response. Consider, for example, the following exchange:

    T: **Kyoo wa nan de gakkoo ni kimasita ka./**

    (S: **Basu de kimasita.**)

    T: **Nan-ban no basu desu ka./**

    In this example, the second question will not work if the student has responded to the first question by saying **Aruite kimasita.** A better second question for T might be something like:

    Dono gurai kakaru n desu ka./

    provided the student has learned this sentence pattern and vocabulary.

4. Make sure that the interview sounds natural as a spoken discourse. Pay attention to the naturalness of each sentence as well as the overall flow of the interview. Avoid long strings of questions, for they usually elicit only short, unconnected answers. (Review content question techniques in Section 2.) Include any body language and movements in the interview, such as standing, sitting, and bowing, that would normally accompany the conversation you are developing. The entire interview should sound and look like natural extended conversation.

5. Do not use structural patterns or vocabulary that the students have not yet learned. This point is especially important for achievement testing of elementary-level learners. Any use of unfamiliar language during test-

ing can make a student nervous and adversely affect overall performance.

6. Begin the interview with some warm-up exchanges (e.g., greetings or comments about the weather) and gradually move to more probing cues.

Eliciting a Meaningful Performance in an Oral Interview

Successfully implementing a prepared interview script in a face-to-face interaction with students requires a skillful performance by the teacher. Some of the factors to keep in mind are the following:

- If possible, conduct the oral interview with a team of two teachers, one conversing with the student, the other keeping a record of the student's performance. The recording teacher should sit in a location that will in no way interfere with the interaction between the student and the teacher conducting the interview. It is also useful to record the interview with a video recorder, audiotape recorder, or, ideally, both.

- Be flexible. Sometimes a student may lead the conversation in directions you had not anticipated. Redirect the interview by taking the current topic to a reasonable closure and introducing your next topic. Avoid abrupt jumps in topics.

- Do not rush the students. Some may not reach the end of the planned script in the allocated amount of time. It is better to leave some of the topics uncovered than to rush through the planned conversation.

- Be engaged in the content of the conversation. Respond to student's utterances verbally or with appropriate body language. It is particularly important for you to monitor your responses when you have to interview a number of students. You may be conducting the same conversation many times, but act as if it were a new experience with each student.

Giving Feedback on an Oral Interview

Shortly after all students have been interviewed, give feedback to the students.

- If you have recorded the interview on audiotape or videotape, have students review their own interviews and prepare comments. Encourage students to correct their own errors.

- Give an overall impressionistic assessment as well as more detailed comments based on component categories such as pronunciation, overall delivery, appropriateness of language, control of structure and vocabulary, and comprehension. Detailed comments should support the overall impression.

- Point out both positive and problematic aspects of the interview performances. When discussing the problem areas in class, give specific suggestions for improvement and have the students perform that segment again with appropriate modification.

- In subsequent classes, review those areas that caused recurring problems.

SECTION 6:
USING CULTURE VIDEOS IN THE LANGUAGE CLASS

In many Japanese-language programs, instructors are expected to teach either achievement culture or informational culture (see Section 3), whether or not they are native speakers of Japanese. This expectation is based on the erroneous assumption that the instructors are equipped to teach these subjects by virtue of their knowledge of the language and their ability to function in Japanese society. This is analogous to assuming that native speakers are also good teachers of their language merely because they speak it, or that anyone who breathes can teach about the human respiratory system. The culture videos in *JSL-MC* were produced by experts in the relevant subject matter. Each is a rich source of information that no single instructor can offer. When you use them, your function is that of a facilitator.

INTEGRATION

Whether or not to incorporate the culture videos as a required component of your Japanese-language curriculum is a decision you have to make. Given that Japanese is one of the most time-consuming languages for English speakers to learn, you may decide to use all class hours for language practice and discussion of behavioral culture, including language. You may select one or two of the videos for viewing and discussion in class and, if possible, make the complete set available to students for watching outside of class. If you include the culture videos as a resource for learning within your program, however, you should allocate class time for discussion. These videos were produced independently of *JSL 1* materials, but it is possible to tie them loosely to some of the lessons of *JSL 1*, as shown in Table 6-1.

Table 6-1
Application of *JSL 1* Lessons to Culture Videos

JSL Lesson	Culture Video	Discussion Topics / Language Practice Areas
3A	"Meiji: Asia's Response to the West"	Topics: Western influence in present-day Japan Origins of loan words in Japanese Language: Loan words and their origins
5B	"Puppeteer's Apprentice (*Bunraku* Puppeteer)"	Topics: Apprenticeship learning; Preservation of art forms Language: Invitation; verbals **miru**, **tukau**, **tukuru**; descriptions using nominals and adjectivals
6A	"Frontier Fisherman"	Topics: Geography of Japan; Family businesses Language: Locations; eating rituals
9B	"Cram School"	Topics: Education in Japan Language: Locations and directions; time
10A	"Reinventing Japan"	Topics: The family in Japanese society; *uchi/soto* Occupation reform movements Language: Family terms; review of time expressions (e.g., **syoowa**, -**nen**)
11B	"An American Portrait (*Sumo* Wrestler)"	Topics: Integration of tradition and innovation Practice and performance Language: Meeting people; *uchi/soto* distinctions; ritualistic expressions
12A	"Inside Japan, Inc."	Topics: Japanese business practice; *keiretsu* Language: Business encounters (introductions, exchange of business cards)
12B	"Woman Soldier"	Topics: Opportunities for women The role of Japan's present-day military Language: Honorific and humble polite expressions; related hierarchical relationships

PROCEDURES FOR DISCUSSION OF CULTURE VIDEOS

Using culture videos for discussion involves three general stages: having a previewing discussion, viewing the video, and having a postviewing discussion. With some culture videos, it is also possible to conduct postviewing discussions in Japanese or to devise a communicative activity in which students use the cultural concepts presented in the culture video.

Previewing Discussion

Provide a worksheet with a set of questions. Sample worksheets are provided later in this section. These questions help students watch the video with a particular focus. The preview questions have to do with basic information about the video, such as the general subject matter, its viewpoint, and the time period it covers. Have the students answer the preview questions based on any general introduction you give them and any information they may already have. Review these questions after watching the video to help sharpen the students' focus.

Viewing the Culture Video

While watching the video, interrupt it as necessary for brief commentary and clarification to keep students focused on the questions to be discussed afterwards. If appropriate, repeat parts of the video that are most relevant to the theme and objectives of the discussion.

Postviewing Discussion

After giving students a few minutes to write their answers to the remaining questions on the worksheet, discuss with the students the salient points and issues presented in the video. Encourage discussion of the Japanese cultural perspectives that are presented in the video. As an optional follow-up assignment, have students write a short summary of or comments about a specific aspect of the video.

Practice Activities in Japanese

You can use some of the information content of the culture video for a few simple activities in Japanese. For example, it is possible to identify the years in which certain historical events took place, locate on the map the places mentioned, and name the countries that were involved. Following are some specific examples suggested for each culture video.

Encourage students to ask you or each other questions in Japanese. Remember, however, that it is strongly inadvisable to introduce items the students have not learned and practiced systematically. If there are some items you feel you must introduce, ensure that there are no more than two or three for each video, and that, once you have introduced them, you reinforce them repeatedly throughout the program, not just in the discussion of culture videos. For beginning students, most of the substantive discussions will have to be conducted in English. Design carefully what few Japanese activities are possible so that they will function as communicative practices and not merely translation exercises. In regular language sessions, incorporate any knowledge students will have gained as a result of seeing and discussing the culture videos.

CULTURE VIDEO TOPICS FOR DISCUSSION AND COMMUNICATIVE PRACTICE

Before you show any of the culture videos, you should watch each one yourself so you can handle classroom discussions effectively. Use the following brief descriptions and those provided in the teacher's guide to *Faces of Japan II* for reference. Depending on the students in your program and their level of competence, you will need to adjust the level of discussion as well as the amount of time you spend on the videos.

Meiji: Asia's Response to the West (*The Pacific Century* #2)

This film depicts the radical transformation of Japan at the beginning of the Meiji Era (1868–1912) from an isolated society ruled by samurai to a modern industrialized nation. In the early seventeenth century, the Tokugawa shogunate began restricting interaction between Japan and other countries, and by 1640, Japan had become totally isolated except for a handful of Dutch, Chinese, and Korean merchants, who brought information about the outside world. Toward the end of the nineteenth century, Russia, England, the Netherlands, and the United States began pressuring Japan to open its ports. The years following 1854, the official end of over 200 years of isolation, were marked by domestic turmoil and were accompanied by a widespread introduction of Western ideas, from political concepts and technology to clothing styles. Japan also began its aggression in China and Korea and other parts of Asia around this time. Japan's victory in the Sino-Japanese War (1894–95), a war fought over control of Korea, changed Japan's attitude toward China from one of respect to one of arrogance. In the Russo-Japanese War (1904–5), a struggle involving Korea and Manchuria, Japan's victory over a Western power had a significant impact on all of Asia. Imperialism and militarism had a resurgence in Japan.

Some key phrases used in the video include:

* **Sonnoo-zyooi** "Revere the emperor, expel the barbarians" (i.e., the Westerners) was a slogan advanced by the samurai of the Satsuma and Chôshû domains, who opposed the opening of Japan. Satsuma and Chôshû correspond to the present-day Kagoshima and Yamaguchi prefectures, respectively.

* **Bunmee-kaika** "Civilization and enlightenment" was a slogan popularized in the early Meiji Era to refer to modernization, largely realized through imitation of anything Western.

- **Hukoku-kyoohee** "Rich nation, strong military" was a slogan promoting industrial growth to strengthen the nation and its armed forces.

The videos also feature some important historical figures whose names are well known in contemporary Japan.[4] Yoshida Shôin was an educator from Chôshû, one of the two domains that opposed accepting Westerners in Japan. He proposed that Japan learn Western technology while keeping the Japanese spirit.

Fukuzawa Yukichi popularized Western culture and believed that commitment to it on a national level would lead to success on an individual level. His portrait is printed on the ¥10,000 bill.

Itô Hirobumi, the first prime minister of the Meiji government, wrote the Meiji Constitution. Natsume Sôseki, a novelist, is considered one of the most influential figures in modern Japanese literature. He raised doubts about the effects of rapid modernization.

In addition to the questions on the worksheet, the following may serve as topics for postviewing discussion:

- How do the ways in which Japanese incorporated Western culture into their lives in the early Meiji period compare with the ways they treat things Western, especially American, today?

- What ideas that were developed during the early Meiji years prevail in present-day Japan?

- What was ironic about Japan's relationship with China in the 1890s?

- In what way was Japan's victory in the Russo-Japanese War a turning point for Japan and Asia?

Along with Western ideas, the Japanese borrowed a number of words from European languages during the

---

[4] Japanese personal names introduced in culture videos are presented with family name first, then the given name.

early Meiji years. Today the Japanese continue to borrow extensively from foreign languages, especially English. With visual aids, identify some common loan words (e.g., **pen, konpyuutaa, miruku**) and identify their origin (**huransugo desita ka./**).

Reinventing Japan (*The Pacific Century* #5)

This video examines the reform policies set during the Allied Occupation of Japan (1945–51) following its defeat in the Second World War, the democratization of Japan, and the subsequent development of the current Japanese economic system.

The extensive reforms introduced by the Occupation authorities at the end of World War II in 1945 included land reform, the dissolution of the *zaibatsu*, a major change in the role of the emperor, demilitarization, the release of communists, the drafting of the new constitution, education reform, and the recognition of civil rights. The new constitution of Japan, drafted by the U.S. reformers, characterized the emperor as the symbol of the state rather than a deity, banned military aggression, and gave women the right to vote and run for public office. The Occupation of Japan ended in 1951 with the signing of the San Francisco Peace Treaty and Japan's agreeing to a U.S. military presence in Japan.

Important figures of the period include General Douglas MacArthur, head of the Occupation forces, and Yoshida Shigeru, the first prime minister of democratic Japan and leader of the Liberal Democratic Party. Yoshida was a conservative industrialist.

Some additional topics for discussion after showing the video are:

- In what ways did the Allied Occupation of Japan "reinvent" Japan?

- How did the Japanese people respond to the changes instituted by the Occupation authorities?

• How did Occupation policies influence Japan's economic progress?

Discussion in Japanese based on this film is extremely difficult given the limited vocabulary of the learners.

Inside Japan, Inc. *(The Pacific Century #6)*

This video describes the emergence of Japan as an economic power between 1960 and 1990 and the resulting strain on U.S.-Japan relations. Following the signing of the U.S.-Japan Security Treaty in 1960, the Liberal Democratic Party (LDP) led Japan to pursue rapid economic growth. Protected by government policies and regulations, Japanese companies invested aggressively in the United States and later in Asia, especially Thailand and Singapore. A widespread labor movement began with the strike of coal miners in Miike (1959–60) and became instrumental in the establishment of lifelong employment in Japanese business.

Major scandals (e.g., the Recruit scandal in 1988 and the Nomura Securities scandal in 1991) revealed close corporate-government relationships, symptomatic of the policymakers' inability to regulate business. Japan in the 1990s has experienced an unstable political structure resulting from the LDP's loss of power coupled with friction among special interest groups. At the same time, Japan is expected to play a more substantial role in the international economy to becoming more involved in international and security issues in the future.

The video introduces some entities that are important in understanding Japan in the post-Occupation years:

• The LDP was the political pillar of Japan, Inc. It pushed the U.S.-Japan Security Treaty, favored large companies, and encouraged company groups (conglomerates) in order to strengthen the financial power of Japanese business.

• The Ministry of International Trade and Industry (MITI) symbolizes the bureaucratic pillar of

Japan, Inc. Its primary responsibilities are to protect, provide financial support to, and regulate Japanese industries. MITI encourages businesses to follow a unified direction.

- *Keiretsu*, the business pillar of Japan, Inc., are groupings of manufacturers, banks, and distributors that provide particular financial support to their member companies.

Some topics for discussion after showing the video, in addition to those listed on the worksheet, might include:

- According to the video, how does capitalism in Japan differ from capitalism in the United States?

- How have politics, businesses, and bureaucrats influenced Japan's economic growth?

- What is a *keiretsu*? What is its economic power in Japan?

- What are some of the problems Japan faces as a result of its dramatic economic growth between 1960 and 1990?

For activities in Japanese, practice such business-related rituals as introductions and the exchange of business cards. Have students assume affiliation with Japanese business firms.

Videos from *Faces of Japan II*

The teacher's guide to *Faces of Japan II* that accompanies these videos is a good source of background information and suggestions for discussion. Sample video worksheets, found later in this section, include questions that are relevant for students in language programs.

Several activities in Japanese are possible in connection with these videos.

• With "Puppeteer's Apprentice, (*Bunraku* Puppeteer)" practice invitations to events (**Ikimasen ka./**), acceptance (**Ii desu ne!**) or rejection (**Tyotto..**), and small talk (**Kinoo mimasita. Kiree desita yo./**).

• For "An American Portrait (*Sumo* Wrestler)," prepare a set of photographs or drawings of *sumo* wrestlers with vital statistics on the back. Have half of the students assume affiliation with the stable to which these wrestlers belong. Have the other students ask them questions about the wrestlers. Students should ask about the characteristics of the wrestlers—for example, who is quick, large, powerful, skillful. The key structure is /**Dare ga** + predicate/. Students should also practice the use of nonquestion comments.

• Following the showing of "Frontier Fisherman" and discussion in English, have students ask you questions in Japanese using a map as on the video worksheet. Use time and place expressions like /place + **kara/made/** and /time + **kara/made/**.

• The video about a young Japanese woman's decision to join the Self-Defense Force, "Woman Soldier," raises some important questions about the role of the military in today's Japan. A possible Japanese activity will take the form of an interview in which the students interview you in the role of Fumiko, the young woman who goes through basic training in the Self-Defense Force (**zieetai**). Encourage students to use the extended predicate in their questions (**Doo site ... n desu ka./**, for example), when appropriate.

• "Cram School" presents another important aspect of Japanese society—education. For practice in Japanese, assume the role of a high school student preparing for an entrance examination, and have students interview you about your daily routine. This will require expressions like the following:

Nan-zi ni gakkoo e ikimasu ka./ Nan-zi made desu ka./

Yobikoo no zyugyoo wa nan-zikan-gurai desu ka./ Mainiti na n desu ka./

Ban nan-zi-goro made benkyoo-suru n desu ka./

Taihen desu nee.

SAMPLE VIDEO WORKSHEETS

The next eight pages present sample worksheets for the culture videos.

Name: _____ Date: _____

Title: " Meiji: Asia's Response to the West" _____

Previewing Questions

1. What key historical events are presented in this video?

2. What time period does this video examine?

Postviewing Questions

3. What significant social conditions existed just before 1868?

4. What kind of phenomena does the word **bunmee-kaika** refer to?

5. Why is the beginning of the Meiji Era (1868–1912) so important in modern Japanese history?

6. What were some of the costs of Japan's rapid modernization?

7. How did Japan's imperialistic militarism begin?

8. How was Japan's relationship with China characterized before the 1880s? After?

Name: _____ Date: _____

Title: " Reinventing Japan" _____

Previewing Questions

1. What key historical events are presented in this video?

2. When did the Second World War end?

3. Who is Douglas MacArthur?

Postviewing Questions

4. What political system did the post–World War II Occupation of Japan by the Allied powers bring about in Japan? What system did it replace?

5. What were some of the missions of the Supreme Commander of the Allied Powers (SCAP)?

6. What impact did the Occupation reforms have on the lives of the Japanese people in the years after the war?

7. What major characteristics of Japan's new constitution does the video mention?

8. In 1947 what events outside of Japan affected the Occupation reforms?

9. What impact did the Korean War have on Japan's economy?

10. In what area did Japan formulate its own unique system, contrary to the plans of the Occupation reformers?

Name: _____ Date: _____

Title: " Inside Japan, Inc." _____

Previewing Questions

1. What is MITI?

2. When did Japan become an economic power in the world?

3. Why is it important to understand Japan's political system when trying to understand its economic system?

Postviewing Questions

4. What entities are the pillars of Japan, Inc.?

5. How did MITI steer Japanese industry toward a focus on electronics in the late 1950s?

6. What two events in 1960 shaped Japan's course of action in the following 30 years?

7. How did Japanese TV manufacturers compete against U.S. TV manufacturers? What role did MITI play?

8. How does the *keiretsu* promote the idea of Japan, Inc.?

9. What are some of the concerns the Japanese people have today about the relentless economic growth the country has pursued?

Name: _____ Date: _____

Title: " Puppeteer's Apprentice (*Bunraku* Puppeteer)" _____

Previewing Questions

1. What is *bunraku*?

2. Who is portrayed in this video?

Postviewing Questions

3. How usual is it for a college graduate to pursue an apprenticeship in a traditional art form such as *bunraku*?

4. What kind of relationship does Minoichiro, the apprentice, have with his master teacher?

5. How large are *bunraku* puppets? How are they handled?

6. What does the apprentice learn about the technique of handling a *bunraku* puppet?

7. What does the apprentice learn about mind and spirit in connection with this traditional art form?

8. What Japanese cultural values are reflected in a *bunraku* performance?

9. How would you compare a puppeteer's training with the training you are undergoing to learn to perform in Japanese communicative contexts?

Name: _____ Date: _____

Title: "An American Portrait (*Sumo* Wrestler)" _____

Previewing Questions

1. What is *sumo*?

2. Who is Konishiki?

Postviewing Questions

3. What kind of relationships do wrestlers in the same stable have with each other during training? during a tournament?

4. Who takes care of the daily needs of Konishiki? How is that assignment of responsibility determined?

5. Why are *sumo* wrestlers typically so big?

6. How structured is the daily life of a *sumo* wrestler? How would you compare a *sumo* wrestler's daily life with that of an American football player?

7. What rituals are observed during a *sumo* tournament? What is their significance?

8. How do traditional and contemporary Japanese culture blend in the world of *sumo*?

Name: _____ Date: _____

Title: " Frontier Fisherman" _____

Previewing Questions

1. Where is Hokkaido?

2. How important is fish in the Japanese diet?

Postviewing Questions

3. Where does Mr. Hamamatsu fish? Locate the area on the map.

4. What kind of responsibilities does Mr. Hamamatsu have?

5. What influence does geographic location have on Mr. Hamamatsu's work?

6. What international issues does the video depict?

7. How involved is Mr. Hamamatsu's family in his business?

8. How do families in a fishing village help each other?

Name: _____ Date: _____

Title: " Woman Soldier" _____

Previewing Questions

1. To what extent does Japan's military participate in international disputes?

2. How common are women soldiers in Japan's military?

Postviewing Questions

3. What is the primary purpose of Japan's Self-Defense Force?

4. What social opportunities does a woman have in Japan's Self-Defense Force? How does this compare with the situation in the U.S. military?

5. What economic opportunities does a woman have in Japan's Self-Defense Force? in the U.S. military?

6. What responsibilities does a woman have in Japan's Self-Defense Force? in the U.S. military?

7. What restrictions does a woman have in Japan's Self-Defense Force? in the U.S. military?

Name: _____ Date: _____

Title: " Cram School" _____

Previewing Questions

1. What is a cram school? Do cram schools exist in the
   United States? For what purpose?

2. How important is education in Japan?

3. What kinds of schools are there in the Japanese
   education system? What are they called in Japanese?
   How many grades does each of these schools typically
   cover?

4. When was the current system of education in Japan
   established?

Postviewing Questions

5. How does Japan's college admission process differ
   from that of the United States?

6. Why is cram school necessary for college entrance?
   What are some criticisms of the Japanese college
   admission process?

7. How important is it for Japanese students to go to
   college?

8. How important is the selection of college in Japanese
   society?

9. How are parents involved in their children's
   education?

SECTION 7:
PACING: SAMPLE HOURLY ASSIGNMENTS

This chapter provides some concrete examples of hourly assignments. It outlines how to structure the very first hour of class, how to combine the various activities of *JSL-MC* in class, how much to cover in a given hour, how to integrate performance in Japanese and discussion about Japanese, and how and when to give quizzes and examinations. How much material to cover in a year of instruction depends on a number of factors, discussed to some extent in Section 1.

The samples of hourly assignments in this chapter assume a program with the following characteristics: (1) classes meet every day for 50 to 60 minutes, with an additional hour or two each week for discussion; (2) students are expected to practice outside of class, using the multimedia tools; and (3) teacher(s) prepare situated, interactional activities for practicing performance in Japanese. You need to adjust this pacing according to the local conditions and goals of your program—in many cases, one or more of the conditions described above are not met. In addition, most introductory programs incorporate reading and writing. In a curriculum that uses *JSL-MC*, written Japanese is best introduced after Lesson 2.

GETTING STARTED

The very first hour should include at least some activities that require students to use Japanese. You also need to give some basic information about the course. Before class, prepare name cards, each with a student's family name, to distribute at the beginning of the class and collect at the end. After a very brief introduction in English about what is going to happen in class that hour, move directly into Japanese, practicing the Classroom Instructions and some of the Greetings and Useful Phrases, both in the Introduction in *JSL 1* and in the CD-ROM program. Use the last 20 minutes for discussion in English about the course.

Hour 1: Introduction and Orientation, Part 1

Classroom Instructions (CIs)

Listen and respond to the instructions with appropriate actions, as modeled by your instructor.

Greetings and Useful Phrases (GUPs) #1, #2, #5

Listen to and repeat the phrases, then practice using them in appropriate contexts, as provided by your instructor.

Discussion: Program goals and materials

Before the next class, listen to CIs and GUPs on the audiotapes or the CD-ROM program to review and prepare.

Classroom Instructions

Classroom Instructions (CIs) are a set of Japanese directives for you to use during all future class hours to manage classroom activities in Japanese. Students are not expected to learn to say these directives, but they must be able to comprehend them and act accordingly. Practice these instructions in the following manner. If you have an assistant, ask the assistant to model what students are supposed to do. Otherwise, designate a spot where you will go when you want to show a model response. Speak at normal speed and move around to make eye contact with students. Move from one student to another quickly, in random order. It will take approximately 20 minutes to introduce all of the CIs.

1. Write on the board, "Where were you born?"

2. Say to your assistant **Kiite kudasai**, and have her put her hands behind her ears, as if she were listening. Repeat this several times.

3. Now say **Kiite kudasai** to one of the students. If the student responds with the correct body language, go on to another student. Repeat this with other students until the desired reaction occurs promptly. Depending on class size, you may or may not be able to have every student respond to this cue at this stage. If only part of the class has a chance to respond, make sure that the other students get their chance at the next step. If a student cannot respond correctly, go back to the assistant or another student who can respond correctly to show the model response, later returning to the student who had difficulty.

4. As you point to the utterance on the board, now say **Itte kudasai** to your assistant, who responds (in English), saying, "Where were you born?" Practice responding to this directive using the same procedures as in step 3.

5. Mix up the first two examples.

6. Introduce **Kotaete kudasai.** The assistant should now tell where she was born (in English). Repeat the procedures of step 3 to practice responding to this directive.

7. Now mix up all the examples introduced thus far. Continue in this manner until you introduce all the CIs.

8. After **X-san ni kiite kudasai** is introduced, give two-phrase instructions: **S1-san, S2-san ni kiite kudasai. S2-san, kotaete kudasai.** This will produce reactions from both S1 and S2. Also include variations like **Moo iti-do kiite kudasai** (variation of **Moo iti-do itte kudasai**), and **Ooki na koe de kotaete kudasai** (variation of **Ooki na koe de hanasite kudasai**).

Note that by addressing the students when giving your instructions, you are already introducing several important features of Japanese interaction: (1) that the students' names have a Japanese pronunciation, (2) that adult students are addressed with their family name, and (3) that you are using the suffix -**san** with names in addressing the students. Be careful not to let the students address you in this hour, since they have not yet learned how to address a teacher.

Greetings and Useful Phrases

Greetings and Useful Phrases (GUPs) are constantly used in everyday interactions and are crucial for students to master. They are introduced in the Introduction to *JSL 1* and in the CD-ROM program without any structural analysis (imagine analyzing "Goodbye" for the beginning learner of English), but the Miscellaneous Notes in the textbook and the Notes in the CD-ROM program provide useful cultural information about how and when they are used. Provide contexts for classroom practice accordingly.

As students have not yet had a chance to listen to the models on the audiotapes or in the CD-ROM program, introduce only a few examples during the first hours. Concentrate on #1, #2, and #5, modeling the phrases and having students repeat them several times, using the following procedures:

1. Show a picture suggesting a time of the day appropriate for a morning greeting (the sun rising, a clock showing 8 a.m., and the like).

2. After saying **Kiite kudasai** to instruct the students to listen, give the model: **Ohayoo gozaimasu**. Repeat the model several times.

3. Now say **Itte kudasai**, followed by **Ohayoo gozaimasu**. Students are now expected to repeat the utterance. If the class is large, move into individual student practice after one or two choral repetitions. Depending on the phrase, it may be necessary to build up the phrase a little at a time, always starting with the end of the sentence. For example, to practice **Ohayoo gozaimasu**, practice **gozaimasu** alone first, then **Ohayoo gozaimasu**. Repeat this with all or most of the students.

4. Continue practicing, but this time add your response. To do this, say **Itte kudasai**, and when the student says

Ohayoo gozaimasu, respond with **Ohayoo**, or
Ohayoo gozaimasu. Repeat this with several students.

5. Reverse the order of speech: Say **Kotaete kudasai**,
followed by **Ohayoo** or **Ohayoo gozaimasu**. Students
must now respond with **Ohayoo gozaimasu** in either
case. Repeat this with several students.

6. Now have two students exchange morning greetings,
both using **Ohayoo**. Repeat with several pairs of
students.

7. Switch the picture to an afternoon greeting, and follow
steps 2 through 6 for **Konniti wa**. For this greeting,
however, there is no variation dependent on the
speaker-addressee relationship.

8. Mix up the two greetings. Depending on the picture
you show, students must distinguish between **Ohayoo
(gozaimasu)** and **Konniti wa**. Prepare self-stick notes
on which you write "Teacher" or "Supervisor" to
practice distinguishing between **Ohayoo** and **Ohayoo
gozaimasu**, depending on the relationship between the
speakers.

9. Introduce **Sayo(o)nara** in the same manner. Combine
Sayo(o)nara with **Ohayoo (gozaimasu)** or **Konniti
wa**.

During this practice, use the CIs appropriately to avoid
resorting to English. End the class with **Sayo(o)nara**.

The second hour is much like the first, but by then,
students will have had a chance to listen to the CIs and
GUPs. The review practice of Classroom Instructions does
not follow the steps described for Hour 1. Instead, use
these CI phrases extensively as you practice GUPs.

Hour 2: GUPs and Orientation, Part 2

GUPs: #3, #4, #18, #19

Follow the same procedures as for Hour 1, but from now on, come to class prepared to PERFORM in Japanese. Practice the assigned utterances with the CD-ROM program or the audiotapes until you can understand them and say them smoothly and accurately. Read all relevant notes and explanations.

Pronunciation Practice (in Introduction): Row 1 and Row 17 (Practice 17b)

This is for pronunciation practice ONLY. Repeat after the model. Do not try to memorize the words or their meanings.

Review: CIs and GUPs #1, #2, #5
Discussion: Responsibilities and requirements
Before the next hour: Listen to all GUPs.

Pronunciation Practice

Both the CD-ROM program and the audiotapes provide pronunciation practice, but the practice drills in the CD-ROM program are easier to use. If students can go over them outside of class, there is no need to spend any class time on any of the specific items. Instead, use the GUPs to practice specific points as they occur. For example, use **Konniti wa** and **Konban wa** to practice the mora **n**.

Orientation

It is, of course, important to give basic information about the course and the program of instruction at the beginning; however, it is more effective to give detailed orientation information to students in smaller chunks, after they have had at least some concrete experience in the target language. Students who attend some classes before deciding to enroll could have a distorted notion of the course if they hear nothing but orientation information during the introductory hours.

Hour 3: GUPs and Orientation, Part 3

Discussion: GUPs

> *Be sure to have listened to all GUPs before class.*

Discussion: Grading policies; learning strategies

The third hour may be conducted in English to go over the cultural points related to GUPs and to complete the course orientation. As part of the discussion of grading and make-up policies, point out that students have the ultimate responsibility in learning, and that the classroom is essentially where they can use the skills they have practiced in realistic communicative settings. Talk about learning strategies and go over the instructions given for Hours 1 and 2. It is important that students have a clear understanding of what is expected of them in terms of preparation for each class hour.

In Hour 4, continue to follow the practice procedures for GUPs as described for Hour 2. Note, however, that the assignment for Hour 2 includes specific instructions on how to prepare for class regularly after that hour—instructions that are not being repeated in Hour 4.

Hour 4: GUPs

Performance: GUPs #15, #6, #7, #8; #14, #20, #10

> *Practice these items by repeating them until you can say them smoothly. Pay careful attention to their meaning.*
>
> *Your instructor will provide contexts in which it is appropriate to use the GUPs you have prepared. Try to learn the association between context and speech: You should be learning when to say what.*
>
> *Do not repeat the CI phrases, but be able to respond to them with appropriate actions.*

Review: All previously introduced GUPs

Pronunciation Practice: Rows 5 and 6; long vs. short vowels

COORDINATING SCRIPT-BASED PERFORMANCE AND APPLICATION

The order of presentation in the textbook is the ideal order to follow when using *JSL 1*. However, when all class practice is based exclusively on the CCs or Utilization, instruction can become tedious for both teachers and learners. By combining CCs of one lesson with the Application Exercises of the previous lesson, for example, it is possible to relieve the potential monotony and also ensure that items are constantly reviewed and integrated in a spiral manner. The following three hours of assignments show this type of combination.

Hour 16: Lessons 1B, 2A

Performance: 2A CCs #9, #10 + Application Exercise B

1B Application Exercise A2 (Drills I, G, K)

1C Utilization #1– #5

For the next class hour: Watch and listen to all CCs in Lesson 2B.

How is your pronunciation? Are you working with the CD-ROM program and tapes?

In Hour 16, the students perform the last two CCs of Lesson 2A. In the same hour, they also engage in extended discourse based on the CCs and Drills of Lesson 1B. To prepare for the particular Application Exercise assigned for this hour (A2), students need to work on Drills I, G, and K in addition to reviewing the CCs in Lesson 1B. They also need to review Sections A and B of Lesson 1 to prepare for the Utilization in Section 1C. When various components are combined in this manner, classroom activity is also broadened. Not only are you using the material from Lesson 1B to do the Application Exercise A2 of that lesson, but you can incorporate in it newly introduced elements of Lesson 2A. In this manner, you help students build a performance repertoire.

Hour 17: Lessons 1B, 2A

Discussion:	2A CCs and Structure
	2B CCs content
Performance:	1C Utilization #6 – #15
Quiz 1B:	Comprehension

      The discussion hour following the conclusion of one set of CCs will also have as topics both the previous set and the new set of CCs. By Hour 17, for example, students will have practiced performing all of the CCs of Lesson 2A, but will have only watched and listened to the CCs of Lesson 2B. Discussion of the CCs of Lesson 2A will have included treatment of the new structures and vocabulary introduced in these conversations, but the discussion of the CCs of Lesson 2B will focus more on the behavioral culture exemplified by these conversations. Students may also have questions about the Drills and Application Exercises in Lesson 1B during this hour. Give them an opportunity to ask these questions before giving the comprehension quiz. See Section 5 for various assessment strategies.

Hour 18: Lessons 2A, 2B

Performance:	2B CCs #1, #2, #3 + Application Exercise B
	2A Application Exercise A1 (Drills B, E, F)

      Hour 18 shows a similar combination of the new and the old.

SECTION 8:
ACTIVITIES FOR ADVANCED STUDENTS:
EXPANDING A DISCOURSE REPERTOIRE

Advanced learners of Japanese may use *JSL-MC* to measure their strengths, to diagnose their weaknesses, and to review the material. Section C of each lesson in the textbook, the audiotapes, and the CD-ROM program are particularly useful for these purposes. Advanced learners can also use the multimedia tools for practice of advanced skills. This chapter outlines three examples of advanced activities designed to expand the types of discourse a learner can handle. These include, in ascending order of difficulty, reporting, restatement, and narrative presentation based on research. The first two activities use CCs, and the third follows the viewing of culture videos.

CC REPORTING

This activity involves reporting on the content of a CC from the point of view of one of the participants. Take, for example, the very first CC in Lesson 1 between Mr. Yamada and Ms. Miller:

(Yamada) **Wakarimasu ka./**

(Miller) **Ee, wakarimasu.**

This conversation can be recast by having the speaker who gathered information in the original conversation (Mr. Yamada) report to another speaker (S2). The resulting conversation might be:

(S2)   (Yamada)

Miraa-san wa huransugo, wakarimasu ka./	**Ee, wakaru soo desu yo./**
	or
	Ee, wakaru tte.
	or
	N, wakaru n da tte.
	or
	Ee, wakaru tte itte (i)masita.
	or
	Ee, wakaru to iu koto desu.

An introductory remark such as **Kinoo kiita n desu kedo** may precede any of these reports. The student who plays the role of Mr. Yamada will have to make a choice from among many possible ways of reporting, based on the relationship between the two speakers and Ms. Miller, on the one hand, and the closeness of the connection Mr. Yamada has to the actual information, on the other.

The following is an example of procedures for this activity using the same CC as a concrete example. It assumes that students are able to handle the directives used in the procedures as well as the various reporting speech possibilities indicated above.

1. Show the video of the selected CC, using either the CC video or the CD-ROM program.

2. Have students identify the speakers (e.g., Mr. Yamada and Ms. Miller are colleagues at the Oriental Trading Company; Ms. Miller is a new staff member) and the location of the conversation (e.g., an office in the Oriental Trading Company).

3. Have one pair of students enact the CC in its original form.

4. If there is a large amount of information to be reported, ask some key content questions to help students remember.

5. Have students take turns assuming the role of Mr. Yamada.

6. Give the remaining students roles to play: They are also employees of the Oriental Trading Company, of about the same rank as Mr. Yamada, but they were not present when this particular conversation between Mr. Yamada and Ms. Miller took place.

Minasan mo, Orientaru-booeki de Yamada-san no dooryoo to site hataraite iru n desu ga, kono hanasi no toki wa, tyoodo soko ni inakatta n desu.

7. Give one of the students, Mr. Brown, a reason for asking the question that Mr. Yamada asked Ms. Miller:

Buraun-san, ano atarasiku haitte kita Miraa-san desu kedo, koo iu huransugo mo wakaru n desyoo ka. Yamada-san ga kiite iru ka mo sirenai kara, Yamada-san ni kiite mite kudasaimasen ka?

8. Have students enact the reporting conversation.

9. Help correct and improve the construction of the conversation, covering sentence structure, vocabulary choice, pronunciation, turn-taking, and listener involvement.

CC RESTATEMENT

CC restatement is similar to CC reporting in that it involves recasting the informational content of a CC in a different interactional mode. Unlike CC reporting, however, one of the participants of the conversation recounts the entire content of the conversation, including contextual information. Using the same example as before, the student who assumes the role of Mr. Yamada has to tell a third person what happened in his encounter with Ms. Miller. The account might be:

Kinoo Miraa-san ga huransugo no hon o yonde iru no o mita n desu yo. Sore de, huransugo ga wakaru no ka tte kiitara,

wakaru tte iu koto de. Ano hito, honto ni iron na koto ga dekite urayamasii desu ne!

The general structure of the restatement will be as follows: It begins with background information as to how the speaker became involved in the conversational interaction in the first place (**Kinoo Miraa-san ga huransugo no hon o yonde iru no o mita n desu yo.**); the conversation itself is then recounted from the current speaker's perspective (**huransugo ga wakaru no ka tte kiitara, wakaru tte iu koto de.**); and finally the speaker's personal comments about anything relevant are added (**Ano hito, honto ni iron na koto ga dekite urayamasii desu ne!**). The three stages should be connected appropriately (**Sore de**) so that the overall restatement forms a coherent discourse. This structure is illustrated in Figure 8-1 below.

Figure 8-1
Discourse Structure of a Restatement

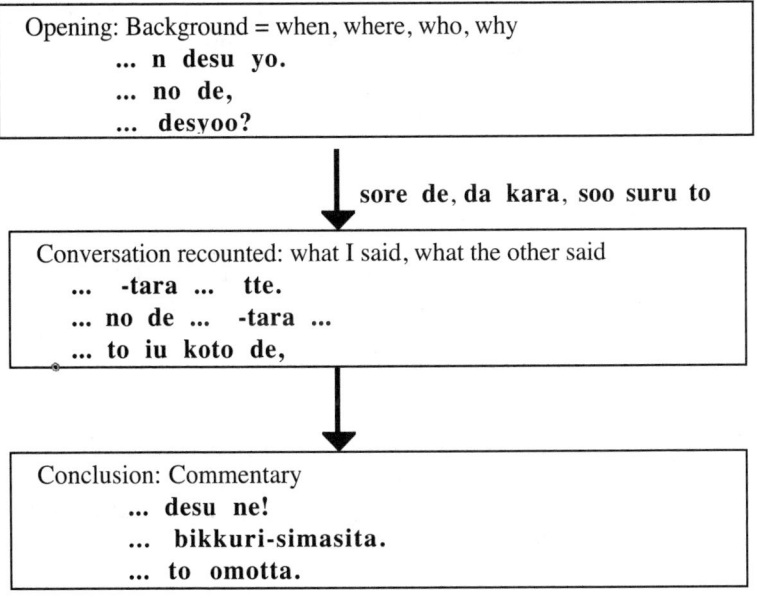

The primary goal of restatement is to develop storytelling abilities. Learners need to use the general discourse structure of Japanese for recounting an event, along with linguistic elements that add cohesion to the overall discourse. They also need to develop narrative skills, including smooth and dynamic delivery and appropriate interaction with the listener in addition to accurate linguistic content. These skills may involve pausing or slowing down at appropriate places, making eye contact with the listener, or adding gestures to engage the listener.

Another important, though less obvious, objective of the restatement exercise is to train learners in listener behavior. Listeners in a Japanese conversation uses *aizuchi*, a constant nodding or use of verbal interjections (**hai, ee, soo desu ka**) at appropriate points in their listening, as a mechanism to signal active participation in the conversation. Since these overt signals for verifying the communication channel occur much more frequently than in English, it is important to train learners in their use and positioning.

The procedures for CC restatement are outlined below, again using Lesson 1A, CC1, as an example.

1. Show the video of the CC that has been selected.

2. Have two students enact the CC in its original form, reinforcing the content of the CC.

3. If needed, ask content questions to further reinforce the informational and interactional content. Note that at this stage, students are talking about the content of the conversation from the point of view of a third party.

4. Assign the storytelling role to students, one at a time. For example, tell a student to assume the role of Mr. Yamada in the example CC. (**Minasan, Yamada-san ni natta to omotte kudasai.**)

5. Assuming the role of an interested third person, provide a reason for the restatement. For example, assuming the role of Mr. Yamada's colleague who has just been introduced to Ms. Miller in the next room, you might say:

Iyaa, ima Miraa-san tte iu atarasii hito ni atta n desu kedo, ano hito, konpyuutaa mo dekiru si, Nihongo mo umai si, sugoi desu ne!

6. Listen to the students' recounting of the CC, giving a model for listener behavior.

7. Suggest correction and improvement as needed. Pay special attention to discourse structure.

8. Have several pairs of students (one pair at a time) initiate the conversation and respond with CC restatement.

9. Suggest correction and improvement in listener behavior as needed. Remember that the proper placement of *aizuchi* requires an understanding of sentence and narrative structure.

PRESENTATIONS BASED ON CULTURE VIDEO TOPICS

Advanced learners may conduct research on aspects of Japanese history, society, or culture treated in the culture videos and present the results in class. Such research is an advanced activity suitable only for students who can engage in extended discourse as well as comprehend and produce written text in Japanese. Specifically, students should be able to handle the basic structure of the language accurately, be able to expand their vocabulary through general interaction, and be familiar with the structure and orthographic conventions of written Japanese. Students need not have read extensively on their research topics in Japanese, but they must be able to conduct interviews in Japanese with Japanese people in the local area to gather data. The basic procedures are as follows:

1. Prepare a worksheet in Japanese similar to those given in English in Section 6 and have students write their answers in Japanese.

2. Have each student select a topic for study. Example topics include:

- Such historical figures as Fukuzawa Yukichi, Natsume Sôseki, Douglas MacArthur, Yoshida Shigeru, or Tanaka Kakuei.

- A place of historical or social significance, such as Chôshû (Yamaguchi prefecture), Hokkaido, the Miike coal mine, or a U.S. military base in Japan.

- Such institutions as a cram school, the Ministry of International Trade and Industry (MITI), or the Self-Defense Force.

- A traditional art form, such as *bunraku* or *sumo*.

- Such social issues as the role of women in Japan's military, characteristics of the education system, or the blending of the traditional and the contemporary.

3. Have students submit a plan for their interviews, including a set of questions they will ask in Japanese and a list of who will be interviewed and why. Suggest changes as needed. Students may plan to ask several people a few questions or one person a number of questions.

4. In class, practice interviewing techniques, including requesting an appointment, expressing thanks, and making other ritualistic exchanges involved in conducting an interview. Practice asking each interview question clearly with an appropriate transition from one question to the next. Practice listener behavior that is effective for the interviewer.

5. Have students conduct their interviews, meeting with Japanese people in the area.

6. Have students submit a written outline of their reports in Japanese. Suggest changes, including stylistic changes, as needed.

7. Have students rehearse the oral presentation of their reports and a question-and-answer session. Demonstrate a model presentation and have students practice set phrases such as:

... ni tuite tyoosa site mimasita.

Soko de, ...

Sono kekka, ... to iu koto ga wakarimasita.

Doo iu koto ka to iimasu to, ...

Naze ka to iimasu to, ...

... de wa nai desyoo ka.

... to (mo) ieru to omoimasu.

... ni tuite ukagaitai no desu ga, ...

... to iu koto desita ga, ...

Pay attention not only to each phrase but also to the structure of the discourse.

8. Have students take turns presenting their reports orally, with a question-and-answer period following each presentation.

9. Have students submit final written reports of their interviews.

Depending on the proficiency level of the students, you may have to stop after step 1. Steps 2 through 9 require a large amount of individual student work outside of class, with class time devoted to advising, practice, and performance.

INDEX

Advanced learners, 9, 92, 97
Annenberg/CPB Project, 6, 7, 8
Application Exercises, 28, 90, 91
Assessing: classroom performance, 54; listening comprehension, 57–58; oral interaction, 54–56, 63; structural understanding, 56–57
Audiocassettes. See *Japanese: The Spoken Language, Part 1 Revised Tape* Series

Body language, 30, 32, 39, 61, 63, 85

Characters in Core Conversations, 6, 38
Cheng & Tsui Company, 5, 6
Classroom Instructions (CIs): for class management, 84, 87; procedures, 84–86
Communicative activities, 15, 28, 30, 51
Communicative interactions, 3, 45
Context: authentic, 27; conversational, 14, 16, 35, 41, 51, 89; establishing, 19, 24, 28, 51; practice in, 20, 29, 86; responding to, 20, 28
Contextualized activities, 46
Contextualized exercises, 2, 12, 19, 29, 56
Core Conversations: Practice; content questioning, 25–28; expansion, 22–24; for building a repertoire of performance, 14; Notes, 15, 18, 39, 42, 86; Setting, 15, 39, 41, 42; Transcription, 42; Translation, 42; variation, 24, 28. *See also* Extended discourse exercises
Correction. *See* Error correction
Course objectives, 34
Course orientation, 83, 88
Culture: achievement, 37, 64; behavioral, 33, 37, 38, 64, 89, 91; informational, 37, 64
Culture videos: for advanced learners, 97; in a language program, 40, 64; postviewing discussion, 66; practice activities in Japanese, 67; previewing discussion, 66; sample worksheets, 75–82; the selection, 7, 40; topics for discussion, 67–74
Curriculum design, 13; local conditions, 14, 83

Discourse exercises. *See* Extended discourse exercises

Discussion: about culture using Core Conversation video, 38–40, 91; about Japanese language, 91; about language learning, 34. *See also* Culture videos

Drills. *See* Assessing, Practice

Equipment, accessibility of, 10, 13
Error correction: avoiding intimidation, 30; by encouraging self-correction, 30, 32, 49; goal, 30; importance of, 31; of pronunciation, 47; timing, 32, 45, 55
Extended discourse exercises: based on culture videos, 97–99; Core Conversation reporting, 92–94; Core Conversation restatement, 94–97; planning and implementing, 28–29, 28, 53

Faces of Japan II video series, 8, 41, 67, 72
Feedback, 54, 58; negative, 30; on an oral interview, 63; positive, 30
Foreign Service Institute (FSI), 3

Grading policies, 89
Greetings and Useful Phrases (GUPs), 86–87

Hammerly, Hector, on culture, 37

Ingroup, 25
Interaction, authentic, 4, 17, 83

Japanese culture, 33, 36, 40, 79
Japanese language: reading and writing, 7, 34, 59, 83; repertoire, 5, 14, 29, 61
Japanese names, 69
Japanese society: communication in, 5, 64; facts about, 41, 65, 82
Japanese: The Spoken Language *Interactive CD-ROM Program*, 4
Japanese: The Spoken Language, Part 1, 5
Japanese: The Spoken Language, Part 1 Revised Tape Series, 5
Japanese: The Spoken Language, Part 1 Video, 6
Japanese: The Spoken Language, Supplement to Part 1—Japanese Typescript, 6
Johnson, Jacquelyn, 8
Jorden, Eleanor Harz, 4, 5, 6

Language program: characteristics, 83; goals, 34, 84
Learners: age, 9; background, 3, 10; responsibility, 1, 35

Learning: lifelong, 3; managing, 3, 45; on one's own, 1, 8, 14; strategies, 3, 34, 35–36, 89
Learning environment, 1, 3
Listening comprehension. *See* Assessing

Macintosh format, CD-ROM program on, 4
Main characters in Core Conversations, 38
Make-up policies, 89
Models for: imitating, 31, 46, 47, 86, 88, 99; responding, 29, 49, 84, 85; Utilization, 51, 53
Models in Context, for Utilization, 51, 53
Mora practice, 88

Noda, Mari, 4, 5, 6

Oral interview: implementing, 62–63; objective, 60; scripting, 60–62
Orientation. *See* Course orientation
Outgroup, 25

Pacific Century video series, 7, 8, 68, 70, 71
Pacific Mountain Network, 8
Pacing the instruction, 83
Parisi, Lynn, 8
PC format, CD-ROM program on, 4
Performance: based on Core Conversation practice, 15, 90, 91; eliciting, 20, 90; monitoring, 30, 45, 59; of interactions, 14, 83. *See also* Record Session Information function
Politeness, 23, 25
Practice: Core Conversation Build-up, 46–47; Core Conversation Role Play, 48; Core Conversation Vocabulary, 46–47; Drills, 48–51, 90; pronunciation, 46, 47, 88; Utilization, 15, 44, 51–53, 54, 59, 90, 91
Pronunciation. *See* Practice
Props, manipulation of, 17, 19, 20, 49, 52, 55

Question and Answer Supplement, A, 6, 56

Reading and writing Japanese, 7, 34, 59, 83
Record Session Information function, accessing data from, 59
Rehearsal, 15
Review: by advanced learners, 9, 92; during Core Conversation practice, 18, 29, 38, 41; need for, 45, 90

Reviewing: Classroom Instructions, 84, 87; cultural information, 66; in spiral fashion, 5, 90; listening comprehension, 58; oral interview performance, 63; structural patterns, 43
Romanization of Japanese, 7, 14

Self-study, 1, 8, 14
Soto. See Outgroup

Teacher's Guide to Faces of Japan II, 67
Teacher's Supplement. See *Japanese: The Spoken Language, Supplement to Part 1—Japanese Typescript*
Teachers, different types of, 33
Testing: achievement, 60, 62; proficiency, 60
Textbook. See *Japanese: The Spoken Language, Part 1*

Uchi. See Ingroup
User's Guide to Japanese: The Spoken Language *Interactive CD-ROM Program*, 4
Utilization, expansion on, 53

Vocabulary, supplementary, 18, 19, 20, 54, 55